Canadian Children's Annual 1980

Editor — Robert F. Nielsen

Art Director — Mary Trach

Potlatch Publications Limited,
One Duke Street,
Hamilton, Ontario L8P 1W9

All writings and illustrations in this book were created by residents of Canada.

Cover painting by D.P. Brown — "Young Canadian" — reproduced by kind permission of the artist.

Frontispiece by Gisele Daigle.

ISBN 0-919676-20-0 (Paperback Edition)
ISBN 0-919676-21-9 (Hardcover Edition)

Printed in Canada.

Table of Contents

The Queen Who Walked On Stilts

by: Thelma H. Foster   *illustrations: William Kimber*

When Elizabelle ascended the throne of Lalapoo, she was determined to be a good queen.

The last king had made the people very unhappy. He had stolen the crown jewels, driven his car on the wrong side of the road, and made silly laws like: school must not be let out until six o'clock, and no one may eat sausage on a Sunday. Everyone was glad to be rid of him.

"I'm going to be a good queen," Elizabelle told her subjects in her first television broadcast. "I will listen to what you have to say, and follow your suggestions. Lalapoo will be a happy country to live in."

"Hurrah for our queen!" cried all the citizens, and they got busy thinking up ideas for their queen to follow.

Next day the queen's advisers came to her. "Your Majesty," they said, "your people say you have such a happy smile. They wish you would always smile."

"Why, that's easy!" exclaimed Elizabelle. "I love to smile. I shall be delighted to please them."

"Hurrah for our smiling queen!" cried the people. "It's like having the sun shining all the time."

A week later, the advisers came again. "Your Majesty, your people would like you always to dress in yellow, because it is like the sunshine."

"What a lovely idea!" cried Elizabelle. "I love yellow. It is the colour of daffodils! I will have the court dressmaker sew up some gowns at once."

It was a lucky thing Lalapoo had coloured television. Before the week was out all the loyal subjects saw their queen in a gorgeous yellow gown covered with lace. In her golden hair she wore a crown of gold set with a large topaz.

The people were in transports of joy.

They cheered and clapped their hands. Some even wept great big tears, although that seems a silly way to show happiness.

Of course not all the suggestions sent in were good ones. The advisers were kept quite busy sorting out the foolish ones and destroying them. But they had nothing else to do. People were so happy they didn't break any laws, make wars, or even gossip about each other. Lalapoo was a fine place to live in.

One day the advisers approached Queen Elizabelle with yet another suggestion. The Prime Minister took off his feathered hat and bowed very low. "Your Majesty, the people would like you to give them a cheering message every day. If you would speak to them at six in the morning, it would send them off to work in a happy mood. Those who find it hard to rise in the morning would spring out of bed to hear your greeting."

"A wise suggestion," said the queen. "It will be a kind of Wake-up Broadcast. You must write me some speeches, Mr. Prime Minister."

"It will be my pleasure, Your Majesty," said the Prime Minister.

The ladies-in-waiting were a little disgruntled when they heard the idea. They grumbled among themselves. "If the Queen is to broadcast at six o'clock, we'll have to be up at five in order to dress her for her television appearance." But of course they couldn't let the queen know they were displeased.

Elizabelle herself wasn't an early riser. She liked to snuggle down for an extra hour in the morning. But her subjects had spoken; she must please them. It would be hard to smile so early in the morning; she felt more inclined to yawn.

The first broadcast was a huge success. How the people clapped and cheered, and skipped off to work!

"Ah!" said the advisers. "Now our country's economy will boom. There's nothing like contented workers to make the wheels of industry run smoothly." And they were so right!

As time went on, Lalapoo became more and more prosperous. Manufactured articles were of such fine workmanship they commanded the highest prices. Trade delegations came from far and near to observe and to learn.

One man who came to observe was a handsome prince from a neighbouring country. He visited Queen Elizabelle in her palace, and was quite taken with her beauty and kindness. Everyone said how wonderful it would be if they should fall in love with each other. But he never popped the question, and his visit ended. However, he didn't leave the country; he moved into the best suite in Lalapoo's biggest hotel.

One day the advisers came with yet another suggestion. "Your Majesty, we have a new request from your subjects. When you go riding in your Rolls-Royce, people line the sidewalks to see you. It is one of their greatest pleasures. However, only those who stand closest can see you. The ones farther back catch only glimpses. Some, in fact, can't see you at all. Now a suggestion has been made that you walk on stilts."

"Stilts!" exclaimed the queen. "I'm sure I should never learn how to walk on them."

"Oh, but Your Majesty! We will have a gymnast show you how. You will learn very quickly. Besides, you will find the exercise healthful and a good example for your people."

The queen smiled her sunny smile. "If my people really wish it, I will try them of course."

Stilts were brought, and the queen practised in a secret arbour, where no one could see her. In a short time she became quite an expert. Grasping them in her lily-white hands, she would give a little bound and she would be off. Thanks to her good sense of balance she never fell down, but strutted around the palace grounds to the great admiration of her courtiers. She was soon ready for a public appearance.

What a perfect day that was! The sun shone brightly, pushing aside the fleecy clouds that sailed over the tree-tops. First came a parade of school children carrying banners, followed by the advisers in a black limousine. Behind them walked Elizabelle on her stilts, her golden hair and yellow dress flapping in the breeze. The people, who could all see her quite plainly, were beside themselves with joy.

"Long live Elizabelle, our beautiful queen!" they shouted.

The handsome prince was there too. He did not wave, but he was heard to say, "What a pity!"

Everything was going nicely. The queen moved gracefully down the street just as though she had been born on stilts. Then something happened. A little boy on the edge of the throng had his Scotty dog with him. Just as the queen was passing, the dog escaped and ran out on the street.

"Come back, Poo-Poo," cried the boy. "Please come back!"

But the dog ran in front of the stilts and tripped Her Majesty. The queen wavered back and forth; then, with a little cry, she fell on the pavement.

"Ooooooooh!" sighed the horrified crowd.

The limousine stopped and the advisers clambered out, shaking with fright.

The queen looked up to see the handsome prince beside her. "Are you hurt, Your Majesty?" he asked, helping her to her feet.

"No, I'm not hurt." Elizabelle looked around. She frowned, pointing at the Prime Minister and his advisers.

"YOU ARE FIRED! And YOU! And YOU! And YOU! Go, and take those silly stilts with you."

"Hurrah!" cried the watching crowd. "How lovely our queen looks when she is angry! Hurrah! Hurrah!"

The queen turned to the prince. "Will you drive me back to the palace? That is, if you know how to drive."

"Of course! I drive my chauffeur around quite often." The prince helped the queen into the limousine. They made a handsome couple as they drove away.

Next day, which was Sunday, the queen held her usual audience from the palace balcony. She wore a GREEN dress trimmed with rubies and pearls! Beside her stood the handsome prince. They both looked very happy.

"My dear people," spoke the queen, "I want you to meet your new king. We will be married on Friday. I won't be able to continue my wake-up broadcasts any longer. But I will show myself here, to my beloved subjects, every Sunday afternoon . . . when the weather is fine. And I promise to smile for you whenever I really feel like smiling."

"Hurrah! Hurrah!" shouted the people, in a frenzy of joy. "Our Queen Elizabelle is the best and wisest queen in the whole wide world!"

And she really was!

Ordeal

by: David Galvin   illustrations: Robin Baird Lewis

With red, roiling rum
  of disquieting scent,
We sailed from Bermuda
  for Stoke-on-the-Trent.
His Majesty's *Nessus*
  with godly intent
Engaged us with volleys
  and calls to repent.

Our pilot, Sam Puffet,
  got shot in the knee
And our sloop steered herself
  to the Sargasso Sea.
"Belay it, me hearties,"
  groaned Cap'n Dundee.
"She'll not make a knot —
  there's no wind in her tree!"

In derelict drift
  on that grotty green sore
Three hundred leagues west
  of the western Azore;
Becalmed at north latitude
  thirty-and-four,
We watched and we waited —
  then waited some more.

The stinks from the seaweed
  were tangible things
That oozed all about us
  in pestilent rings.
The night came upon us
  with hellish hot wings,
And mock-making stars
  seemed to jiggle on strings.

Then fiery freights passed us
   with dead, demon crews —
With Frenchmen and Dutchmen
   and wind-jammer Jews.
Then ghost-glutted galleons,
   broken in twos,
Bore starving men lunching
   on leathery shoes.

A fortnight we skulked
   and we scuttled below.
Till our braids and our beards
   were as white as the snow;
While kraken-eyed, naugahyde
   sea monsters' toes
Would tap on the bow
   in the phosphorus glow.

Then the cabin boy croaked,
   "We've a chance out of ten!"
As he led a procession
   of rum-running men.
And we poured rancid rum
   in the seaweedy fen
Till the weeds shrivelled up
   from the blasphemous blend.

St. Elmo in Heaven
   at last heard our plea:
He sent down a wind
   that could slide the sloop free.
And toasting salvation
   with tankards of tea,
We cursed our farewells
   at the Sargasso Sea.

The Last Afternoon

by: William Ettridge   illustrations: Barbara Eidlitz

The names of fifty birds are hidden in this story. The first, DIPPER, is underlined as an example. Can you find the rest?

"A quick <u>dip per</u>haps?" Eric asked.

"I think not." His cousin scowled at the sea gleaming in the sunlight.

"How about a sail?" he suggested; the sight of a small steamer puffing across the bay prompted the thought. He pointed to his small boat, its masts tilting as it tugged against its mooring. "Shall we, Pam?"

"Very well." She sounded bored. Heading for the quay she led the way, Eric trailing behind.

Girls! he thought. Always wallowing in self-pity.

Moving ahead he jumped into the cockpit. Trying to entice a smile he held out his hand. "Come, climb into my magic rowboat."

A rueful grin curled her lips. "Sorry I was so gruff. It's just that I hate the last day of vacations." With an awkward jump she climbed on board.

In very short order Eric cast off, set the jib, issued Pam with a life jacket, slipped another on his own shoulders, and set sail.

"Which way shall we go?" Eric ducked as the boom swung from one side to the other.

"I don't mind." Pam dug in her pocket for a coin. "I'll spin. Tails we go south, heads, north."

"There's rough water to the north," Eric warned. "Last trip I pitched and tossed about for hours."

"Can't be helped; heads it is." Pam

was much happier now.

Eric chuckled his pleasure. "You'll do. Very well, north we go." He swung the boat round and the sail ballooned swiftly in the following breeze.

One foot hooked under the flag-rack, leaning far out, thoughts wandering, Pam

small arduous ape. I'll feed you to the lobsters — their claws nip easily through little horrid girls."

Eventually they turned for home; it really had been a fun afternoon. Back at the mooring Eric checked every bolt and nut. Hatches battened down to his satisfaction, they set off for the holiday cottage, Pam humming, birds singing in the hedges as they passed by.

Pam's mother met them at the cottage door.

"Did you have a good time, Pam?"

"We averaged a laugh a minute." Pam smiled happily. "I'm so glad we could steal that last boat ride."

"I'm pleased, pet. Reliable and good fun, there's not many boys like Eric."

Pam nodded her head in agreement, eyes twinkling. The thought of returning to school on Monday no longer brought sighs of regret. Her bitterness had completely flown.

playfully scooted her hand through the water. She felt very brave nearing the area of rocks and broken water, sure of Eric's ability.

"Gee! Sensational! Splendiferous!" She shouted her pleasure as the boat pitched wildly. "Isn't it a lark?"

"Hang on tightly now," Eric warned.

Her red-gold hair reminding him of a flaming orange in the bright sun, Eric thought she looked like some viking fisherman of long ago — he called out and told her so.

"Don't be smart!" Inhaling a mouthful of spray her breath rushed out with a splutter. She pulled herself inboard and shook her fist playfully. "I'll have you marched off in chains," she threatened. "Better still, I'll have you tied down by your hair like Gulliver in his travels!"

His side throbbing from laughing so much, Eric wagged his finger. "Why, you low renegade! Pirates of your type we expect to be impertinent, but this is mutiny! You're like an old wooden spar, rotten to the core, and only fit to be thrown over the side. I'll make you walk the plank."

"You don't frighten me, monkey-face. I'll walk it easily."

"Monkey-face?" Eric squeaked as he crossed his eyes in a funny expression. "Listen,

Bird names in alphabetical order:

Bittern	Nuthatch
Crow	Owl
Coot	Parrot
Duck	Petrel
Dove	Pewee
Dipper	Pintail
Eagle	Pipit
Egret	Puffin
Finch	Rail
Flamingo	Raven
Geese	Redhead
Grackle	Robin
Gull	Roc
Hawk	Ruff
Hummingbird	Snipe
Heron	Sparrow
Ibis	Stilt
Kingfisher	Swallow
Kite	Swan
Knot	Swift
Lark	Teal
Loon	Thrush
Mallard	Tit
Martin	Weaver
Myna	Wren

Birdland
by: Barbara Eidlitz

Can you name the 18 types of birds in the painting?
(They all appear in "The Last Afternoon.")

(See answers page 176)

Broomtails

by: Dorothy Blunden   illustrations: Don Inman

What has four legs, lives in the foothills of the Rocky Mountains, steals horses and can run as fast as a truck?

A Broomtail, of course!

In the 1800's thousands of these free creatures roamed the prairies and the coast of British Columbia. Their history was unclear. Some people said they were stray Indian ponies, others thought they were pack horses abandoned by fur traders, while a few folks maintained the horses were a breed by themselves with an unknown origin.

Wherever they came from, they were almost impossible to capture.

Led by stallions, large bands roamed their territory, grazing on prairie grasses and resting in the shade of evergreens. Moving with the wind and snow, they found their shelter in the outcrops of rocks and the denseness of forests.

As more and more people settled in the West, the Broomtails moved closer to the mountains. Their stocky, often short-legged bodies travelled the same routes year after year, crossing and recrossing the mountain streams. Sometimes they would break down fences and trample crops on their way to watering holes. Occasionally they stopped to graze on hay left drying in the fields. But their worst crime was to call to the young mares owned by hard working ranchers and lead them away to travel with the wild herds.

The early ranchers studied the habits of the wild horses. Then in the spring, when the horses were at their weakest, the ranchers acted. They built funnel-shaped corrals of wood or rope-netting in narrow, rocky parts of the Broomtails'

favourite trails. One or two ranchers would circle behind the herd and then, with a yell, rush toward the animals, frightening them and forcing them to run along the trail and into the corral.

The youngest captives were sometimes kept and broken for use on the ranches. One or two strong stallions were occasionally sold to rodeos for bucking horses, but most of the animals were sold to local horse dealers and pet food manufacturers.

Today these scruffy, unshod, unshorn creatures with long-shaped heads and bushy tails still roam the foothills of the Rockies. Their numbers are few but their stamina and toughness are still as great as their ancestors.

Lone stallions still creep close to the ranches seeking to build a herd. Young mares still disappear into the forest, and fences are mysteriously knocked down.

Ranchers, now banned by law from holding roundups, must chase the intruders back to the forests of the high country. Rather than risk crippling their own horses on long chases, many ranchers choose to move the Broomtails with trucks or snowmobiles. In fact, Broomtails have been clocked at speeds up to 45 kph as they raced along bumpy ranch roads trying to escape mans' inventions.

A sign of days past, the Broomtail still leaves man wondering where he came from, how he survives and whether or not he should be protected — or rounded up forever.

Ghosts and Wild Horses

by: Joyce C. Barkhouse

photos: NFB Photothèque and Nova Scotia Communications
and Information Centre

A storm howls across the North Atlantic, and wild horses huddle together in the shelter of a towering sand dune on lonely Sable Island. Their long tails and manes stream in the wind which blasts sand and snow into their thick, protective pelts, and their heads droop as they wait patiently for the blizzard to end.

At last a white-faced stallion stirs and steps away from the others, testing the wind. With a shrill whicker he gives the signal, and leads the way down to the watering-place.

A small, freshwater lake lies in the centre of the treeless island. The horses go to an inlet, and rearing up on their hind legs, come smashing down with their forefeet on the snow-laden ice. Again and again they stamp until a wide opening is made, and they drink together. Then they move away, looking for a pasture where the wind has swept the wiry grass free from snow.

They are a tough breed, these little horses. For hundreds of years their ancestors have survived the winters in this bleak environment.

Where did the first horses come from? Some say they were left there by early Spanish or French colonists who planned to return for them, but their ships were lost at sea. Others say the horses were survivors of shipwrecks. Perhaps the breed was improved by the unplanned arrival of such horses, though usually they were penned and close-tied on deck, and would have had little chance of survival.

Many strange stories have been told about Sable Island, haunted by the sad ghosts of thousands of people who have been shipwrecked on its low-lying shores. It is well named the "Graveyard of the Atlantic." Sometimes the ever-shifting sands uncover — and then cover again — human skulls and bones.

It is difficult to draw a proper map of the island — situated more than a hundred miles off the coast of Nova Scotia — because it is always changing size and shape. From the air it is sickle-shaped, like a new moon. Less than a mile across at the widest, it is about sixteen miles long, but once it was much larger. Sable Island is like an iceberg; only the tip shows. Treacherous sand bars stretch twenty miles or more at either end, just under the surface of the water; it is on these that so many sailing ships have crashed to their doom.

Sable Island is a noisy place. Even on calm days there is the constant booming of breakers, and when a wind springs up, or a sudden, violent storm, the noise is deafening. A man who lived in a life-saving station described a storm:

Suddenly a dull, leaden haze obscures the sun, clouds gather from all directions. The sky assumes a wild, unusual appearance. The wind begins to rise in fitful gusts, carrying swirls of sand before it. The darkness increases as the low, driving sand shuts out all distant objects. Now the gale bursts in awful fury, whipping off the summits of the hummocks, carrying before it a cloud of blinding sanddrift. Darkness adds to the horror of the scene, while the rain descends in a perfect deluge. No human voice can be heard above the tempest. The crinkled

*lightning for an instant lights up the mad
waves, as they rear and leap along the beach.
Then a sudden calm ensues. A few short
gusts at first break this period of tranquillity
and in a few minutes the hurricane bursts
again from the opposite quarter. The
darkness is still intense, relieved only by the
red glare of the lightning, which is quickly
followed by the crashing of the thunder, as it
strives to be heard above the howling of the
blast. Gradually the storm ceases, the clouds
break and pack away in dense black masses
to leeward, and the sea alone retains its wild
tumult.*

It is during such storms, people say,
that ghosts roam the sands. One wraith mourns
and complains in French about his king, Henry
IV, who banished the man's wife to Sable.
Another is one of the murderers of the Portuguese
King Charles, who escaped to Sable to live out his
days in misery. His ghost wears a broad-brimmed
hat, and sings psalms through his nose. But the
most famous of all is the ghost of Mrs. Copeland.

She was first seen by Lieutenant
Torrens, who was himself shipwrecked on the
island. He found a hut, which other survivors had
built out of pieces of lost ships, and had furnished
with a table and chairs and other comforts
salvaged from wrecks. That night he went for a
walk, and when he came back he was amazed to
see a lady sitting beside the fire. Her long,
dripping hair hung over her shoulders, and her
face was as pale as death. She wore only a soiled
white dress, wet from the sea.

"Good heavens, madam!" he ex-
claimed. "Who are you, and where did you come
from?"

She did not answer, but held up one
hand; Torrens saw that one of her fingers had
been cut off and the stump was dripping blood.
He looked around to find something for a ban-
dage, and in that moment she slipped past him
and through the door. He ran after her, but she
ran swiftly and went head foremost into the lake;
when he arrived on the shore he could find no
trace of her. Not knowing what else to do he
returned to the hut, and there she was again,
sitting by the fire! When he went in she held up
her mutilated hand — and then he recognized her
as a person he knew.

"Why, Mrs. Copeland, it's you!" he
cried.

She bowed her head and again held
up her hand, showing the horrible wound. Finally,

Lieutenant Torrens understood.

"I have it," said he. "Murdered for the sake of your ring!"

Again she bowed her head, slipped past him and disappeared.

When Lieutenant Torrens got back to Nova Scotia he talked about his experience. Mrs. Copeland, the wife of a Halifax doctor, had been well-known and well-liked, and her death — apparently by drowning — had been widely mourned. She had been aboard the *Frances*, wrecked on Sable in 1799.

In those days vicious pirates — called "wreckers" — sometimes deliberately lured ships to their doom by lighting false beacons on lonely, dangerous shores. Uninhabited Sable Island was a favourite place for wreckers. They would wait until a ship had been dashed to pieces, and then collect everything valuable that washed ashore. They robbed the bodies of the dead. Did they also attack the living? The story of Mrs. Copeland's ghost convinced many people that they did.

In the early 1800's a life-saving station was established on Sable Island to help castaways, and from that time the island has always been inhabited.

For many years the men who worked as life-savers patrolled the island on horseback; the horses they rode were the wild ones, caught and trained for the task. They were neither very big nor very handsome, but they were sturdy and sure-footed as they trotted over the shifting sand dunes. And they were not at all frightened by the great, thunderous waves breaking on the beaches.

In the old days horses were sometimes taken off the island — as many as fifty at a time — and sold in Nova Scotia, usually to work underground as "pit ponies" in the coal mines. This was a cruel fate for wild creatures who had always roamed free.

Nowadays the horses are protected by law. In fact, nobody is allowed to go to Sable Island without special permission from the Canadian government. Some big companies are looking for oil around Sable, and the men who work on the oil rigs must promise not to disturb wild life.

Probably the ghosts can look out for themselves.

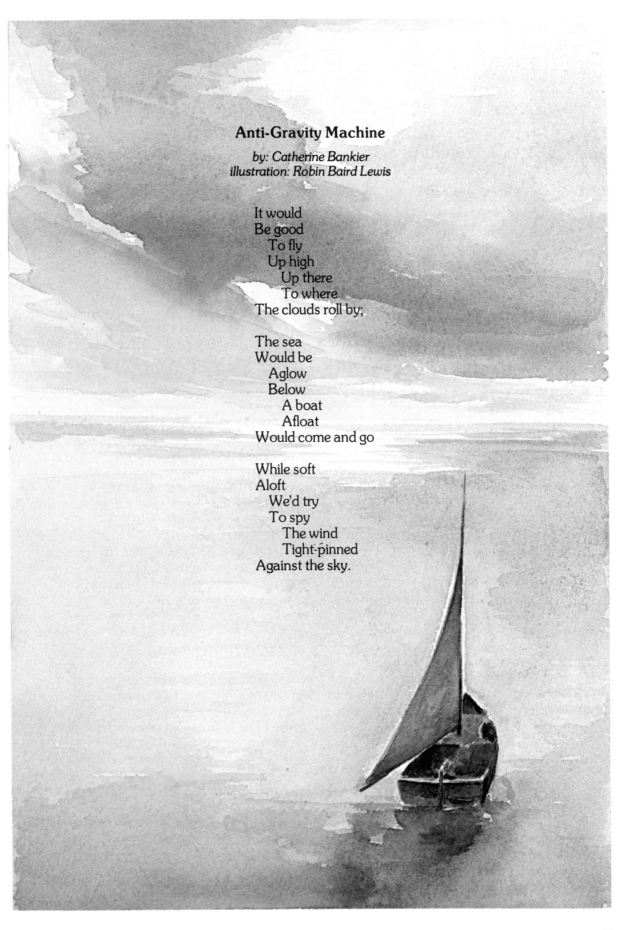

Anti-Gravity Machine

by: Catherine Bankier
illustration: Robin Baird Lewis

It would
Be good
  To fly
  Up high
    Up there
    To where
The clouds roll by;

The sea
Would be
  Aglow
  Below
    A boat
    Afloat
Would come and go

While soft
Aloft
  We'd try
  To spy
    The wind
    Tight-pinned
Against the sky.

The Removal Of Sasha McKlusky

by: Valerie Keller   illustrations: Robin Baird Lewis

If you followed the old river road past the town reservoir over Bryon's Hill and back down into the valley, you came to an unbelievably cluttered yard in the center of which leaned a building that almost defied description.

It had been built, or contrived, with great ingenuity from cardboard packing cases, odd boards picked up here and there, and the whole covered over with the ends of various sized tin cans.

On the sagging gatepost hung a hand painted sign proclaiming that this was the abode of S. McKlusky.

Sasha McKlusky was a short, rotund fellow of indeterminate years, with a bushy metallic grey beard and shoulder length hair to match. His eyebrows were darker, thick and hung down over small black eyes that could dance with mischief one moment and be sparkling with rage the next.

His clothing consisted of a pair of ragged denim coveralls and a red plaid shirt, neither of them appearing to get dirtier or more ragged through the years. For winter, he added a long black overcoat with two rows of shiny brass buttons down the front. Whatever the state of the rest of his attire, those buttons always gleamed.

It was a constant irritation to us as children that an empty bottle or pop can never touched the ground, it seemed, before Sasha had spirited it into his dirty gunny sack. No matter how early we got up on a Sunday morning, Sasha had beaten us to it and the River Road and Bryon's Hill were litter free.

For all his odd ways, and our annoyance over the bottle business, we never were tempted to make him a figure of fun. Sasha seemed to command and receive a reluctant respect from everyone, from the smallest, most ragged kid to the pillars of the town.

The year I was twelve progress hit Greenfields, in the shape of an oil refinery. With it came the related businesses, then larger stores and of course subdivisions.

A developer moved into town and set up an impressive office on Main Street and soon a huge sign board appeared at the edge of town, depicting rolling green river banks on which nestled tiny white bungalows. Above this scene of pastoral serenity were big black letters announcing to the world that River Bend Estates were open to view and purchase.

In actual fact, River Bend Estates consisted of pegs driven into the ground with orange plastic streamers fluttering from their tips.

People drove down River Bend Road, over Bryon's Hill, took one look at Sasha's house nestling in its clump of stunted willows on the edge of River Bend Estates, and went elsewhere for a lot.

The established residents of Greenfields watched with undisguised interest as other small developments sprung up east and west of town and even on the rocky hills to the north. The only things developing along River Road were the weeds that grew up to hide the small stakes and their fading ribbons.

Mr. Marcus Turner, the owner and manager of River Bend Realty, was a tall, heavily built man of obvious means, since he smoked large cigars, drove a gleaming black Cadillac, dressed in impeccable suits and ignored the lesser mortals of the town.

The town waited with bated breath as Mr. Turner set about the removal of Sasha McKlusky.

Of course no one but Mr. Turner and Sasha knew what went on at their interviews, but speculations flew fast and furiously as with increasing frequency the black car stirred up the dust on River Road and jerked to an irritated halt in front of the sagging gate.

Summer turned to fall and still Sasha could be seen imperturbably puttering about in his cluttered yard or dragging his gunny sack along the roads as he searched for treasure, and Mr. Turner could be seen standing on the steps of his office, irritably puffing huge clouds of cigar smoke into the air or sitting morosely in his car watching the weeds going to seed on the River Bend lots.

When Sasha appeared in town to do his meager shopping, he parried inquiries as to his health and how his business dealings with Marcus Turner were coming along with unintelligible grunts and sly winks.

One chilly fall day we saw the big car slide to a halt at Sasha's gate. Determined to find out what was happening, we slithered through the willows and tins, intent on reaching the one window of Sasha's house. Suddenly, right under my nose, appeared a pair of worn but highly polished boots.

A soft and familiar voice said, "Get out of here, you young devils."

We got.

Christmas came and went and everyone huddled around their stoves as the prairie winter raged across the land. Building slowed and finally stopped.

And then, unbelievably, it was spring.

With the warmer weather interest revived in the silent war between Mr. Turner and Sasha McKlusky.

Then, one early April morning, Sasha appeared on Main Street and the populace stared. It certainly wasn't unusual to see Sasha on the streets, but what had everyone agog was the fact that he was minus his sack and was all but unrecognizable with his hair and beard neatly trimmed and wearing a rusty black suit instead of his usual apparel.

Mr. Turner appeared in the doorway of his office and, after a moment of stupefied amazement, broke into a grin of triumph. As he ushered Sasha inside, the street suddenly teemed with life. Small groups formed and reformed across the street and stared avidly at the closed door and shuttered windows of the realty office.

Excitement mounted as my father hurried from his law office, to be followed a few moments later by Mr. Whyte from the bank.

That day the school rooms buzzed and hummed with excited whispers of speculation. Even the teachers had gleams of eager curiosity in their eyes and made excuses to visit each other as the afternoon crawled by.

We were pulling for Sasha, for with the building of houses along the river banks our adventures would be sadly curtailed.

When the three-thirty bell finally rang, four of us streaked from the school, well in the lead of the curious mob, and pelted down the hill to Main Street. It was back to normal in many respects; a few shoppers drifted from store to store and dust devils stirred in the street. But one thing was not normal. Usually Mr. Turner stood in magnificent importance surveying the town from his steps at this time of day, but today there was no sign of him. The black car glistened silently at the curb and the windows of the realty office showed a blank facade to the street.

For awhile we hung around hoping for some development, but finally, muttering disappointedly, we scuffed our feet in the dust and wondered what to do next. Someone suggested we go down to Sasha's, but we knew it would be a long walk for nothing. Sasha kept his own council and, while he wasn't averse to telling us stories if he was in the mood, he wasn't likely to confide in four scruffy school boys whom he considered "young devils" at the best of times.

Glumly we headed for home.

Father was late for supper that night, which was a surprising and disturbing first for he was a punctual man.

It certainly was a day for surprises, for when he finally entered the front door and slowly set his briefcase on the cobbler's bench in the hall, we all stared in amazement.

His usually calm and dignified face wore a look of stunned disbelief.

He looked around at us as though he had never seen us before.

"What on earth has happened, James?" Mother's voice seemed to echo shrilly in the tense silence of the hall.

Father shook his head, for all the world like a boxer who has been punched once too often.

"Sasha McKlusky bought out Marcus Turner's holdings in Greenfields today and turned over the deed to the town." He sank wearily onto the bench and ran a hand over his chin. "There were stipulations." Father chuckled and glanced

at me. "A parcel of it, on the west side, as far from Sasha's place as possible, is to be developed into a recreation area for the children. Sasha said, 'The young devils need more to do than spy on a harmless old man.' There are to be baseball diamonds, soccer fields, an open air swimming pool and even tennis courts."

"What happens to the rest of it?" Mother asked.

"It's to be a wild life sanctuary. Sasha said that way he may get some peace."

"I wish you could have seen Will Whyte, Jane." He looked up at Mother and grinned. "He was a study, I can tell you! That old rascal has a bank account in Edmonton that made Marcus Turner look like a pauper. It must have been even more of a shock to Will than for the rest of us. When he partially revived, he began calling Sasha 'Mr. McKlusky'."

Father rose stiffly to his feet. "Is dinner ready, Jane? I'm starved."

Ignoring Mother's injunctions and a rumbling stomach I rushed out to share the news. I'd always known that Sasha had a soft spot for boys . . . and girls too I suppose.

The Fisherman and the Hunter

by: Dorothy Cameron Smith   illustrations: Susan Cook

Hoderi was a great fisherman in Japan. His younger brother, Hoori, was a great hunter. One day, they decided to change about. Hoderi decided to hunt and Hoori decided to fish.

The older brother, Hoderi, was very angry when he returned from his hunting trip without any game. He threw the bow and arrows he had borrowed down in front of Hoori.

"These are useless!" Hoderi shouted. "They are no good at all. They are poorly made."

Hoori's feelings were hurt. He had spent long hours making the bow and arrows. They were his pride and joy. Hoori bent down to pick them up from the *tatami*, a woven rush mat laid over the floor. "I'm sorry," he said. "I didn't have any luck fishing, either. Perhaps it is wiser to do what one knows best."

"Give me back my fishhook!" Hoderi demanded, his anger still flaring.

Hoori trembled. However, he bravely said, "I lost your fishhook. But I will get you a new one."

Hoderi was not satisfied. "I don't want a new fishhook." Blazing with more anger, he yelled, "I want my old one back again!"

The next day Hoori brought him a *furoshiki*, a square cloth used to wrap and carry things. It was filled with many fishhooks. Hoderi went on hollering.

"Get me my old fishhook! Don't come back until you find it!"

Hoori left his brother and went down to the seashore. There was much grief in his heart. A kind old man appeared. His name was Shiko-tsutsu no Oji, meaning Salt-Sea-Elder.

"Why are you so sad?" he asked Hoori.

The young man told him his story.

"Grieve no more!" the old man implored. "I will look after the matter for you."

Shiko-tsutsu no Oji made a basket

and they climbed into it, sinking into the sea. When they had descended deep down in the water, they reached a beautiful strand rich with all manner of strange seaweed. Stepping out of the basket, the old man led Hoori to the palace of the Sea God.

It was an impressive palace. There were many turrets and stately towers. A cassia-tree bloomed at the gate, and under it stood a lovely young girl. Her name was Toyo-tama, meaning A Precious Jewel.

At first Toyo-tama was frightened of the stranger, Hoori. But when Shiko, the Sea Elder, introduced him and the three of them talked together, the girl lost her shyness.

She smiled with pleasure. "I will take you to my father, the Sea God," she said to Hoori.

Hoori was made welcome at the palace. The Sea God commanded every fish in his kingdom to appear before him. Each fish swam in line and awaited its turn to be inspected.

"Kora! Kora!" the Sea God said, which means, "Here! Here!" Then he spoke a form of poetry in Japan called *tanka*, a verse having thirty-one syllables.

"Kora, Kora,
open up your mouth, good fish,
let me take a careful look.
Hoori has a wish to find
his brother's lost fishhook."

Finally, the fishhook was found in the mouth of the *tai*, the Red-Woman fish. She certainly felt more comfortable when the fishhook was removed.

"Oya! Oya!" the Sea God exclaimed, a way of showing his feeling of success. "We will have a feast to celebrate." He ordered a dish of *akano ghan* to be prepared for the occasion. It was rice with *azuki*, small red beans.

Toyo-tama wore a kimono of fine silk, a magnificent rose colour, and she presented

Hoori with the *magatama* she wore around her neck. It was a claw-shaped stone bead used in necklaces worn by royalty. The Sea God knew then that his daughter loved Hoori. He blessed their marriage.

For three years Hoori lived at the palace. But Toyo-tama knew that her husband missed his earthly home and his brother. She went to her father and told him of her fears. The Sea God was always courteous and kind, and he realized his daughter wanted Hoori to be happy. They both decided to send the young man back to his home.

The Sea God presented Hoori with the Jewel Of The Flowing Tide and the Jewel Of The Ebbing Tide. By dipping it into the water, Hoori would be able to control the sea.

"*Sayonara*," Toyo-tama said to Hoori, which means, "Goodbye."

When Hoori reached his home, he found that his brother, Hoderi, had long since forgiven him. He was overjoyed to see Hoori. Through the years Toyo-tama visited her dear husband, but she always went back to the sea that she knew best. She presented him with a son who grew up to become the father of Kamu-Yamato-Iware-Biko, the first human Emperor of Japan, known as Jimmu Tenno.

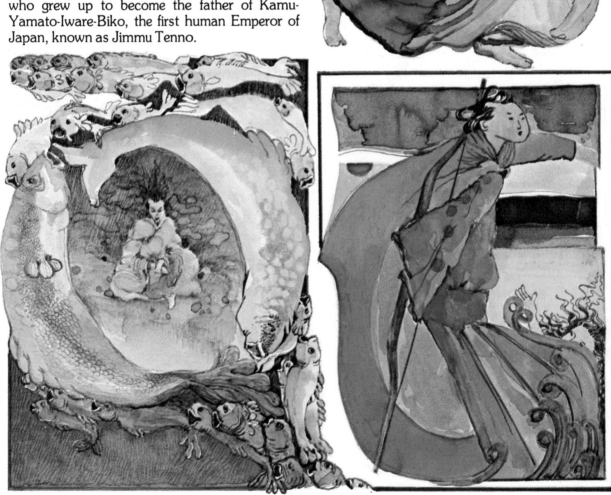

The King of South Pipsissewa

by: Alan Bradley   illustrations: Robin Baird Lewis

The King of South Pipsissewa was not a happy man
Although he'd lots of castles, towns and villages and
land,
And lakes and rivers, orchards, and a splendid marble
throne;
But the people didn't like him so he spent his time
alone.

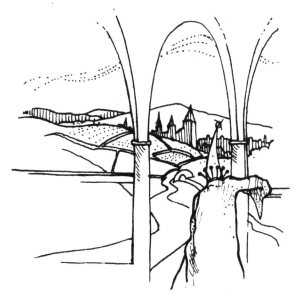

He walked upon the parapets in winter's fiercest squalls
And said aloud while pacing through his lonely Royal Halls,
"I've given them a holiday — the Seventh of July,
But they laugh and point their fingers still whenever I come by."

"I've given them a Court of Law, I've given them a jail,
I've given them a Sheriff with the right to set their bail,
I've given them a convict-ship with handcuffs by the
pair,
And yet they jibe and shout at me — it really isn't fair."

A sudden inspiration came, His Highness dried a tear:
"I'll call the Kingdom's Wisest Man to tell my why
they jeer."

The Wisest Man was summoned and he
scratched his ancient head

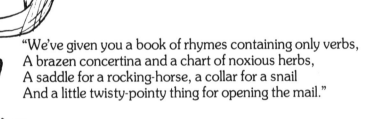

As he heard the King's complaint he sighed, and this is what
he said:
"We've given you a clockwork snake that slithers up a string,
A lens to look at termites with, a toad that's taught to sing,
A lantern for projecting backwards pictures on the wall
And a whistle with the pea removed that makes no noise at
all."

"We've given you a book of rhymes containing only verbs,
A brazen concertina and a chart of noxious herbs,
A saddle for a rocking-horse, a collar for a snail
And a little twisty-pointy thing for opening the mail."

"We've given you some gum-boots and a motto for your
wall,
A container so that walking-sticks won't clutter up your hall,
A prism that's for looking through, a paperweight of gold
And a cut-out card of sheep — or ships, depending where
you fold."

32

"We've given you a bird's nest and a shark without a fin,
A nightingale that's made of glass, a weathervane of tin,
A swimming pool for goldfish and a spool of yellow thread
And a comforter of goosey-down to keep you warm in bed."

"You've given us a thousand things — but gifts we cannot bear.
One thing you *haven't* given us — and that one thing is care."
The Royal Face grew red and dark in truly Royal Rage
And he summoned Royal Soldiers who locked up the Royal Sage.

The King of South Pipsissewa was not a happy man
Although he'd lots of castles, towns and villages and land,
And lakes and rivers, orchards, and a splendid marble throne;
But the people didn't like him so he spent his time alone.

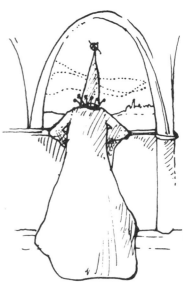

33

She Hates Me, She Hates Me Not

by: Griselda Christmas   illustrations: *Nancy Lou Reynolds*

On a sunny morning in mid-May a girl pedalled furiously along a suburban road, on an old bicycle that was too small for her long legs. Her short, blonde hair blew untidily in the breeze as she headed for Chase's Riding Academy, two miles from her house, on the outskirts of the city.

Alice Marshall was, as usual, later than she had intended. It was the morning of the first horse show of the season, and she knew it would take her close to an hour to groom and braid her grey Anglo-Arab mare, Misty. She had meant to be at the stable by seven-thirty, and here it was, nearly eight already. Crimson catfish, Alice thought, peering at her watch. Oh well, plenty of time, really, and at least I didn't forget anything.

She glanced with satisfaction at the carrier basket of her bicycle. In it, partially protected by a torn plastic bag, were her black jacket, crash cap, white stock tie, and gloves, while three carrots, an apple, and a hamburger bun bounced precariously on top. She was wearing her tan breeches and riding boots, an uncomfortable costume for bicycling, so that Alice was feeling hot and dusty as she panted along the final stretch and wobbled across the gravel of the stable yard.

The double doors at either end of the big barn were wide open, and even from the yard Alice could hear the shrill clamour of excited children. John Chase, the imperturbable ex-jockey who ran the stable, taught his pupils not only how to ride, but how to groom, clean, and feed, as well as elementary first aid for the numerous ills and mishaps which beset horses. Therefore, at eight o'clock on this show morning, there were fifteen children of various ages all trying to groom and braid manes and tails at the same time.

Alice hastily propped her bicycle against the outside wall and, grabbing a carrot, plunged energetically into the melee, shouting, "Hi, everybody. Morning, John."

Several voices responded to her greeting, and John, critically overseeing the labours of a small boy with his pony's tail, looked up with faint disapproval.

"You're late, then."

"As usual," Alice responded cheerfully. "Mum and Dad are away for a week, and that lazy brother of mine wouldn't wake up to drive me."

She peered over the door of a box stall beside her, where a plump, round-faced girl was polishing a sturdy bay horse with an old towel.

"Hi, Gwen. Almost finished?"

Gwen Adams turned, shaking horse hairs out of her cloth.

"It's about time you got here, lazybones. Better skip the chatter and get cracking."

"Hey, would you believe I had to bike? You'll come and help me, won't you?"

"You gotta be kidding! I haven't even started Rusty's mane yet."

"That won't take long. Rusty's so easy to do — he stands still."

"Well, okay," Gwen agreed good-temperedly, pushing mouse brown hair off her face with a forearm. "If I'm finished in time. Here, take my brush; the others are all being used."

"Thanks, pal." Alice seized the brush and hurried down the passage to the box stall where her fidgety little mare, ears pricked expectantly, was waiting for her usual titbit.

Alice affectionately straightened the wild black forelock.

"Hello, my little pet. Greedy girl, want your carrot?" As Misty crunched, she slipped the halter over the mare's head, and ran her hand down the smooth, grey neck. "Crimson catfish, you — are — a — mess. How do you get so dirty?"

She set to work vigorously with curry comb and brush, and was soon working in a cloud of dust and floating white hairs. After a while she stopped, wiping her hot face with the sleeve of her shirt. "That's rather lick-and-a-promise, pet," she told the horse, "but it'll have to do. I don't suppose anyone'll notice. Now for your braids. Where did I put my elastics? Help, don't tell me I didn't — Oh no, here they are."

Putting some elastic bands between her lips, she first dipped the brush in water and damped the mare's mane; then, dividing it into sections, she started to plait. Misty, excited by the uproar around her, was alternately titupping around the stall and thrusting her head impetuously over the half door, ears pricked, to see what was going on. Alice hung on to a piece of her mane, saying forbidden words thickly through a mouthful of elastics.

Gwen, finished with her own horse, came to stand outside the stall.

"Tch, tch," she teased. "A big, strong girl like you, an athlete, captain of all those school teams, and you can't manage your own horse!"

Alice said "Grr" through clenched teeth, and succeeded in fastening another braid. "Don't needle me, Gwen Adams, or I might just blow up and

34

bust." The mare made another circle, and Alice scrambled after her.

"Why don't you tie her?" Gwen asked.

"You know I can't. She panics. Oh, crackling crimson catfish, stand still!"

Gwen gaped. "Crackling what? That's a new one!"

"Crackling crimson catfish," Alice repeated complacently. "I thought of it the other night when I couldn't do my algebra and needed something really fierce."

"It's fierce all right." The girls stared at each other poker-faced for a minute before exploding into loud laughter. Misty side-stepped rapidly and Alice lost the braid she had just completed.

"See if you can hold her," she begged.

With Gwen's help the last hair was finally folded more or less neatly into place and fastened with an elastic.

"No tail?" Gwen asked.

"Bother the tail. Lots of people don't do tails any more. I'm tired."

Alice shut the door of the loose box and flopped on a bench in the passage.

"Man, what a life! Here it is not even nine and I feel as though I'd been working for hours."

"Mum will be here soon with the trailer," Gwen said, sitting beside her, "but we can relax for a little while."

The two girls sat without talking, watching other people scurry around like agitated ants, still not ready. Alice was nervous, a rare experience, and it bothered her when she stopped to think about it, like a

headache hovering in the background. She was uneasily wondering if her chief rival, her enemy, that detestable little Nancy Warren, would be at the show. Maybe it's too early in the season, she thought. Maybe she hasn't trained enough, maybe she's given up riding. What a hope! Idiot, why do you let it bug you?

Gwen interrupted her brooding. "You know you've got smudges all over your shirt?"

Alice leapt impatiently to her feet. "Oh, who cares? My jacket will cover them."

She peered at Misty to make sure she was still neat and tidy, and walked restlessly down the passage towards Gwen's horse, Rusty.

"I hate this waiting around," she grumbled.

Gwen trailed after her, still talking about shirts. "I use one of Dad's cast-offs over mine, like a sort of smock."

"Oh, you're so organized," Alice snapped, and was immediately sorry. "Rusty looks absolutely gorgeous," she offered by way of apology.

They watched the stable's five small ponies being led out, one by one, and loaded into a truck. A harassed father, who had volunteered to chauffeur their riders, was distractedly trying to herd the children into his car, but they kept wandering away. Alice absent-mindedly collared a little boy, who was running into the stable for the third time, and headed him in the right direction.

"You don't need it, whatever it is," she told him firmly.

A dusty station wagon pulling a rattling two-horse trailer turned into the stable yard.

"Here's Mum," Gwen called. "Let's collect our tack first."

Suddenly full of energy, they ran inside. Alice slung the saddle over her arm and, picking up the bridle, remembered her clothes in the carrier. The bicycle had fallen over and the plastic bag lay on the ground, its contents spilled in the dust. "Suffering snakes," Alice muttered crossly, "I hope Mrs. Adams has a clothes brush."

The back of the car was occupied by a lively and undisciplined Sealyham terrier, who yapped steadily and scrabbled at the windows.

"For goodness' sake, don't let Chips out," Mrs. Adams warned. "He'll fight with John's dogs for sure."

Gwen tossed her load in quickly and went to help her mother let down the ramp. Alice, with both hands full, shoved her saddle against the little dog's whiskery face.

"If you were mine . . . Boy!" she threatened grimly.

The horses loaded easily; even the unreliable Misty, conscious of Mrs. Adams a wary distance behind her with a raised broom, walked on with only a few dramatic snorts and trembles.

"She's not really afraid," Alice explained, "but it's against her principles to give in too easily."

Holding Chips firmly by the collar, the girls settled themselves in the car.

"I'll sit in the back, shall I," Alice suggested. "And guard our jackets and things against Chips." She was feeling much more cheerful now that they were on their way.

"Why, he won't touch your clothes," Mrs. Adams said, surprised.

Gwen giggled. "Mother dear, don't you remember last year, going to Aylmer, when he was so quiet all the way, and we found when we got there that

he'd spent all his time taking Alice's stock out of its plastic bag and chewing the end?"

"Oh. Yes. H'mm. I'd forgotten that. But he was only a puppy then. He doesn't chew things now."

"What, never?"

"Well, hardly ever," came the chorused reply, and they all laughed.

"I'll sit here anyway," Alice decided. "Honestly, by the time I've groomed and braided I feel so hot and dirty, and my boots are all dusty."

"Well, if you'd only . . ."

"Never mind, don't say it. 'Wear an old shirt like I do.' Actually it's a good idea, but I always forget. By the way, have you got a clothes brush? My jacket fell in the dirt."

Gwen grinned and said, "Typical!" as she handed back a small brush from the glove compartment. Alice scrubbed at her jacket, which by now showed dog hairs as well as dust. She considered the result doubtfully with her head on one side, pursed her lips, and said, "Oh well, good enough."

They had to travel only about fifteen miles, but it took them half an hour because Mrs. Adams drove so carefully.

"I'm sure the trailer is going to come unhitched one of these days, it's so old."

"Darling Mrs. Adams, I don't know what we'd do without you," Alice said, pert but sincere, at the same time giving Chips a surreptitious jab with her elbow to keep him off her lap.

They slowly negotiated the last sharp turn into the fairgrounds and stopped beside several other trailers at one side of the parking lot.

"The first class hasn't started yet, so we have lots of time to warm up," Gwen said with satisfaction.

"M-m," Alice answered vaguely, busy looking all around to see if her enemy, Nancy, had arrived.

The field beside the ring was dotted with trailers and trucks. Everywhere ramps were being lowered and horses backed out. Some children had already mounted and were trotting around, while others were agitatedly giving a final polish to sleek, rounded flanks. Not many spectators had arrived as yet, and Alice could see the ring, empty and waiting, with the jumps stacked at one side, immaculate and sparkling in their fresh, start-of-the-season paint.

"What are you looking for?" Gwen asked.

"Nothing special. Wait, Gwen, let me get Misty's bridle on before you take Rusty out."

There was no sign of Nancy. Alice bundled her uneasy feelings into the back of her mind and, with the efficiency of long practice, slipped the bridle over Misty's high flung head.

"Okay," she called.

Gwen unhooked the chain behind the mare and Alice backed her out onto the grass, where she stood staring around suspiciously, bug-eyed with excitement. Suddenly realizing that there was grass, she began to eat as though famished. Gwen unloaded Rusty, who came out quietly, as placid and cheerful as his mistress.

"Alice, are you letting her *eat?* Your bit will be all green."

"I know, but it keeps her quiet."

Mrs. Adams laughed. "You're like the mothers who let their kids stay glued to the boob tube all day long, to keep them out of the way." She climbed out of the car, slamming the door upon the terrier's hysterical yapping.

"Drat the dog!" she muttered, lighting a cigarette. "Gwen, where is Chip's leash?"

"I don't know, Mother."

"Oh, here it is. I'll take him for a walk and get your numbers for you," she offered, opening the car door with the leash ready to clip on the dog's collar. Chips leapt past her and darted off, giving tongue shrilly as he went.

"Chips!" Mrs. Adams screamed, hurrying in pursuit. "Come here, you wretched dog!"

Alice laughed and picked up her saddle. She was just about to put it on the mare when a new landrover with a matching trailer pulled into the show grounds and stopped not far away. Alice's heart jumped into her throat and pounded uncomfortably.

"I knew it!" she exclaimed bitterly. "It's her, it's Nancy! Is she going to pester me all this summer, too?"

Gwen walked closer, towing a reluctant horse.

"Oh man, is that cool! I wish we had an outfit like that."

"Miserable little creep, I suppose she's going to win everything again, with her two thousand dollar thoroughbred and her fancy groom." Alice's usually pretty and cheerful face looked sullen as she watched a small, dark girl get out of the landrover and go around to the trailer.

Gwen looked unhappily at her friend. "She's not really a creep, Allie, just because her people have money —"

"I think she's a creep," Alice retorted viciously. "She can't *do* anything, she can't play any games, she can only study, and anyway, any moron could win with a horse like that."

"She can ride, though. She's good," Gwen replied. Then, not wishing to quarrel with Alice, whom she had admired and followed faithfully for years, she suggested cheerfully, "Let's get saddled up. Our equitation is the second class, and then the junior working hunter."

"She'll be in all the same classes. She should be showing that horse conformation, not working."

"She probably would if there were a conformation class in this show, which there isn't." Gwen turned away and lifted her saddle flap, poking her horse sharply in the ribs. "Breathe out, Fatso," she commanded, and tightened the girths.

Mrs. Adams arrived with the girls'

numbers gripped in one hand, strings fluttering in the breeze. With the other hand she dragged Chips on the end of his leash.

"I got him," she announced triumphantly. "Here you are, Alice. Number twenty-five."

"Oh, thanks." With the reins looped over her arm, Alice absent-mindedly dropped her number on the ground, and began to saddle her mare. Nancy, Nancy, always Nancy, she thought resentfully. Everywhere I go, there she is, too. Why can't she go and do something different? Why is she always in my way? Why doesn't she just go and drop dead? This was ridiculous, and Alice knew it, but she went on deliberately, recalling in luxurious detail every grievance she had stored up for months. She remembered the first day Nancy Warren came to school, at the beginning of the summer term, a year ago. The girls had clustered around after classes, asking her questions, Alice, as usual, taking a leading part.

"Why're you starting school now? Where do you come from?" they asked.

"We just moved from Montreal," Nancy said. She was a small, dark girl, delicate looking and rather shy, but with a sweet, friendly smile. "My father was transferred, and we moved right after Easter."

"You're not French, are you?" Alice asked.

"No, actually we were only there for a couple of years. Before that we lived right here in Ottawa, but on the other side of town."

"You only look about twelve years old. How come you're in our class?"

"I'm fourteen."

"Huh!" Alice was half jeering. Something about the smaller girl interested and yet irritated her; perhaps it was the meek, quiet manner. Carelessly she continued to tease Nancy, and the other girls followed her lead. The newcomer lost her eager expression and began to answer nervously.

"Do you play basketball?" Alice asked.

"N-no, not very well."

"How about tennis?"

"A bit, I guess."

"Volleyball? Soccer?"

Nancy shook her head.

"Swimming? I guess you study a lot, don't you?"

"Not such a lot."

"Just naturally brainy." Alice grinned around at the other girls, tossing her blonde hair. "Well, what *do* you do?"

Nancy looked miserable. She bent her head, and the soft, dark hair slid forward, hiding her face. "I guess I ride a lot," she said in a low voice.

"Ride!" Alice turned away, flabbergasted. Was this puny and pale-faced little creature going to challenge her in her own special field?

That summer Nancy proved to be more than a challenge. She was a disaster. Lonely and unwanted, she put her whole heart into her riding, and won far more often in the shows than impatient, slapdash Alice. She won ribbons, but no friends. Alice had set the fashion of disliking Nancy, and so far nobody had bothered to change it.

The whole of the following winter Alice, uneasily conscious of the other girl, charged through school activities with greater gusto than ever. She played harder, talked more loudly, and ran the Junior Athletic Committee with vigour, but was never able to ignore the quiet girl who drifted around like a shadow, and, like a shadow, was always present.

"It's weird," Alice complained, glancing uneasily over her shoulder as she and Gwen were walking down the corridor. "She haunts me. She follows me around."

Gwen gazed at her in surprise. "Well we all go to the same classes, don't we?" she pointed out.

Alice could not explain. She wished she had never started the silly game of bait-the-new-girl. Now, unable to forget or ignore Nancy, Alice felt that everywhere she went, everywhere she looked, she saw

that pale face and timid smile. Exasperation and jealousy had grown into real hatred.

Now, when Alice saw Nancy drive up, she realized that this new showing season might be a repetition of last year, if not worse. The thought made her seethe with rage and resentment. Mounting Misty, she started schooling in slow circles, but her mood infected the horse, who bounced and cantered sideways, fighting for her head. Alice lost her temper,

as much with herself as with Misty, but the damage was done, and the horse was soon thoroughly upset.

When the equitation class was called, Alice was sure she had no hope of winning; she was too much out of harmony with her mount. However she was still, quite obviously, a strong and competent rider; after the preliminary walk, trot and canter both ways of the ring, she found herself and five others, Nancy among them, kept back while the rest of the class was dismissed.

Now for the individual work, Alice thought. I've still got a chance, but I wish I'd done more schooling. She listened carefully to the judge's instructions, repeating them in her mind. Sit-trot in a figure eight, strong trot up one side. Halt. Rein back. Canter back in a straight line, first on one lead, then on the other. Halt. Nothing difficult, if only I can keep Misty in hand. I mustn't let her get away from me.

She made the mare stand quietly while the others were being tested one by one, hoping that the wait would calm her. Watching each rider gloomily, she decided that they were all good, although two of them could not make their horses canter on the off lead, and one had no extended trot. Nancy's horse worked like a machine. Pushbutton trained, Alice thought scornfully.

When it was her turn, she made a conscious effort to relax. Misty started nicely. Her sit-trot was a little quick, but she was supple, and bent easily in either direction. However she leapt too eagerly into an extended gait. Crackling crimson, Alice thought, that's not the way. She's not stretching her legs, she's just moving them faster. Now she won't halt properly. Whoa, Misty, easy, pet. Now you can canter — not too fast, darn it. Alice was losing her temper again, but she tried not to show it. Only the horse knew; she slanted her ears back anxiously, and bounced.

Alice patted and soothed Misty when they finished, but inside she was boiling with rage. She knew she had not done as well as Nancy, and the judge thought the same, for he gave Nancy first place, and Alice fourth.

Gwen was waiting for her at the gate.

"Nice going, kid," she called cheerfully, but Alice scowled.

"It wasn't good at all. I was doing everything wrong."

"Nonsense. Absolute boloney. Come and look at the jumping course. It's posted over here."

Leading both horses, they pushed their way into a group of riders clustered around the notice board, and examined the diagram of the course with care.

"Not too bad," Alice mused. "Just a plain figure eight. Let's see — brush and cedar rail up one side, diagonally down here, chicken coop and garden gate. That's a new one. Then the other diagonal — birch rails in-and-out and an oxer, and then down the last side, more rails and a wall. Hey, sharpish turns, eh?"

"They've never had a garden gate before. That's kind of tricky."

"It's awfully narrow. Look, they're putting it up now." Alice stood on tiptoe, trying to see into the ring. "It's got brush on both sides, and sort of posts, with the little gate in the middle. Betcha we jump the brush part, and not the gate."

"Betcha we don't jump it at all. Gosh, I wish John had better jumps at the stable, for schooling."

"Can't be helped now. Let's get our positions. I hope I can go second. I like to get it over with, and then I can relax and watch the others."

"Not me. I'd rather go at the end."

The second place in the order of jumping was taken, but Alice got the third. It was a very large class. "Over forty entries," the steward told them.

Alice groaned. "It'll take all day," but Gwen was happy. "With that many kids, there are bound to be some worse than me. I'll go fifteenth — that's a good lucky number."

Alice mounted and trotted off to put her horse over the practice jump. Misty, eager and excited, flew over the jump and charged off with her head down. Alice had to sit down and pull her in hard.

"I can stop you all right, my girl, but it looks terrible," she muttered grimly, and went to the collecting ring to watch the first competitor.

Three refusals. Good! Alice thought ungenerously. That gets rid of him pretty quickly. One more to go. Come on, kid, get with it.

The second entry, a fat child on a fat pony, was doing a slow round. The pony knew all about it, as ponies always do, and moreover had its own idea of what the course should be. Straight around the outside it lolloped, ignoring alike the jumps in the middle and its rider's despairing tugs and cries. At the end it collapsed thankfully into a walk, and ambled out of the ring with a self-satisfied expression, as much as to say, "What's all the fuss about? I did it, didn't I?"

Alice giggled nervously. "That's a perfect cartoon by Thelwell," she remarked aloud.

Misty entered the ring snorting and dancing, but still went quietly enough up the first side and around the turn at the top. Alice felt hopeful. "Good girl," she encouraged. "You're doing fine; now you *mustn't* stop at the gate."

Misty pricked her ears suspiciously at the odd looking jump, and Alice, feeling her hesitate, used her legs hard. Too hard.

"Oh, crackling crimson *catfish!*" she exclaimed in despair as the horse took off like a rocket.

Sitting down hard, trying to regain control as they scrambled around the next corner, she soothed Misty as well as she could with hand and voice. "Whoa, girl, whoa then, easy." The pace was much too fast for the in-and-out, and Misty muddled the stride in the middle, knocking down the second half of the jump. Sure-footed as a cat, she skipped over the rolling poles, but was sufficiently off balance to bring down the next jump as well. Around the last corner Alice managed to get control again, but it was too late, and she left the ring with eight faults.

"That's the absolute *end,*" she told herself, disgusted. "I should put her in a steeplechase. Either that, or learn to ride properly."

Having walked the mare until she was cool, Alice shut her in the trailer, and strolled disconsolately over to the rail, where she watched Gwen happily give a mediocre performance on a reluctant horse.

Mrs. Adams came and stood beside her.

"Hard luck, dear," she said. "You were going a good clip, weren't you?"

"Much too fast," Alice agreed, resting her elbows on the top rail, and thrusting both hands into her already tousled hair.

"Oh well, it's fun anyway, isn't it? Alice, honey, would you be an angel and hold Chips for me? I want to talk to Gwen." Without waiting for an answer, Mrs. Adams handed the dog's leash to the girl and walked away.

Alice looked down at the restless dog with dislike. "You'll darn well behave yourself if you stay with me," she told it savagely. As Chips strained at the leash, uttering strangled yelps, she gave him a slap and said "Sit down!" The terrier, looking startled, obeyed her promptly. "There now, all you need is a bit of discipline."

She forgot the dog and returned to watching the competitors critically. It was certainly a big class. There must be more than forty kids, Alice thought. Too many. The shows are getting much too slow. They'll have to limit the entries somehow — perhaps have more small schooling shows, or separate hunter trials, or something.

Nancy was one of the last to enter the ring. She sat easily on her chestnut thoroughbred, and her hands were quiet; on a horse, she seemed to acquire authority. Darn it, Alice thought, she *is* a good rider. I hate her.

Alice was standing beside the wall, which, at three foot six, was the highest jump. Chips, bored again, was wriggling around and pulling on his leash, but Alice paid him no attention. Her whole mind was concentrated on Nancy, willing her horse to make a mistake, to misjudge a take-off, to fumble a landing, anything so that her hated rival would not win. "But she's going perfectly," Alice muttered. "Oh damn, damn, damn!"

Now Nancy was approaching the wall, was only two strides away. Without any conscious thought, Alice loosened her grip on the leash, and Chips was in the ring, running, yapping, straight in front of the horse. There was a confusion of thudding hooves, the horse was down on its knees, and Nancy was flung hard against the wall, where she lay very still.

Alice stood without movement, paralyzed by horror. The little dog crept back under the rail, ears and whiskers drooping, and Alice picked up his leash. She felt frozen — turned to stone — but inside a voice was crying out in agony, "I didn't mean to, I didn't, I didn't!" And then, very faintly, "Did I?"

Somebody caught the horse and led it away while the first aid men were bending over Nancy. She was sitting up. Alice closed her eyes for a moment and saw, as though written across her eyelids, "Not dead." Of course she's not dead. "Shut up!" she ordered the crying voice inside her, and looked again.

Nancy was being helped to her feet. The men were supporting her left arm bent stiffly across her chest; she was very pale, but she never made a sound. The crowd too, after the initial gasp, had been silent, but now, as Nancy left the ring, there was an outburst of clapping and some calls of "Brave girl!"

After a few moments Alice turned and wandered vaguely back to the car, looking dazed. Chips had recovered his bounce sufficiently to hurl himself with bristling threats at a passing collie, but Alice yanked him back fiercely.

"It's all your fault, you stupid little . . ." She flung him into the car. "I ought to clobber you," she snarled, and glared into the whiskery little face which peered at her apprehensively through the window. For a minute they held this pose and then, with a gesture of despair, Alice sat on the front seat and put her hand on Chip's rough back. The dog flinched, but she soothed him.

"It's all right, Chips. You can't help being a yappy little pest, can you? It's my fault, all my fault. I let you go. Oh dear God!" Alice covered her face with both hands. "I didn't let you go on purpose, did I? I didn't, I'm sure I didn't. You pulled away." Sensing her misery, as dogs will, Chips sat quietly beside her, and she held his warm, panting body tightly, staring blindly at nothing.

Gwen found them like that when she arrived a moment later.

"Oh, Allie, what happened? It was Chips, wasn't it?"

Alice nodded.

"Did he get away from you? Honestly, he's awful. I don't know why Mum can't make him behave. He's always in trouble."

Alice suddenly turned to Gwen and grasped her arm.

"Gwen, I didn't mean to, honestly I didn't. It just happened by mistake, didn't it?"

She looked distraught and desperate. Gwen stared at her.

"Well of course you didn't *mean* to. Don't be silly, Allie. Of *course* it was a mistake!"

Alice still sat, staring.

"Come on, girl, snap out of it." Gwen shook her gently. "It was an accident — just one of those things. People are always falling off, and at least the horse didn't step on her."

"The horse!" Alice cried, suddenly leaping up. "Was the horse hurt? I'll go and see — no, no use. Her man will look after it."

"Listen here," Gwen said firmly, taking her arm. "No, leave that stupid dog in the car. Nancy has a broken arm, probably, and that's not too bad. Her horse hasn't a mark on it, but it's time your horse had some lunch, and mine, and us too. So come on, you've got work to do."

All the rest of that day Alice remained withdrawn, aloof, while the pageant of the show flowed about her. Classes were called, judged, and dismissed. Horses snorted and whinnied, tossed restless heads or drooped patiently. The loud speaker blared the names of entries, children saddled, unsaddled, shouted, laughed, or complained. The sun shone, faces grew red and sweaty, the ground was littered with discarded paper cups, but Alice moved within her own private cloud, her mind clamped fiercely down upon the fear deep inside. Perhaps later on, perhaps when she was alone, she would be able to raise the lid from those dark thoughts, and let them out carefully, slowly, to be assessed one by one. That way she might cope, but not here, not now.

She responded briefly to Gwen's cheerful chatter. She rode in two more classes, feeling a long way off from her body, as though she were watching

some other girl. She even saw that girl win a second and a third place ribbon, but felt only a dull, detached astonishment.

By the time they got the horses home and settled in their stable with a warm mash for each of them, it was after seven in the evening. Alice did not want to talk to anyone. The numbness was beginning to wear off, and she felt raw and sensitive all over, as though even the touch of a feather would make her shrink. The stable was full of children eagerly doing a post-mortem on the day's events, but Alice avoided them and bicycled slowly home.

Her parents were away and her brother, in the den, was insulated from the world inside a cocoon of loud music from the record player. I don't suppose he even knows I'm here, Alice thought, wandering into the kitchen. She stared vaguely for a while at the refrigerator, then opened it and poured a glass of milk, which she placed on the counter. Should I eat? she wondered. Cold chicken? Cheese? Ugh! She shut the door and, forgetting about the milk, crept upstairs to her bed.

Just to be alone — Alice felt that if she could only crawl beneath the covers, bury herself like a wounded animal in a hole, maybe it would all go away. If she slept, it would be all right in the morning — just a bad dream. Well, sleep then, she told herself. You're tired, so sleep. But she couldn't. She kept hearing the thud as Nancy's body hit the wooden wall, and seeing the crumpled figure lying on the ground. Then back to the beginning again — the picture of herself standing there, letting the leash slip. Had her conscious mind told her fingers to let go? Or was it simply an accident? Oh yes, it was an accident. Oh please, God, let it be an accident!

Restlessly she turned on her back, staring with burning eyes into the darkness, then to her side again, burying her face in the pillow. She began to remember other scenes — all the times she had been mean to Nancy, done cruel things — why had she behaved like that? The time she was standing on the school steps with a group of girls, and Nancy had come out, slipped on some ice and sat down, and they had all laughed, not like friends, but jeering. And the time she had, giggling, persuaded the high school hero, the quarterback of the senior football team, to approach Nancy and say, "Would you like to go to the dance on Saturday night?" And when Nancy looked up, blushing with surprise, and said, "Why, yes," he answered, "Well I hope someone asks you."

How mean could you get? How cruel! Alice writhed with shame, and clenched her fists. How,

how, how could she have done that? And the boy was utterly horrible to have gone along with the trick. And there were other things — looks, and giggles, and petty remarks passed to the girls. Oh why couldn't she fall asleep and forget all this? But Alice knew, after hours of tossing and turning, that she would never forget it. I'll have to do something, she told herself hopelessly — make it up to her somehow. At least I can talk to her, apologize — I could crawl like a worm in the mud if it would do any good. I'll go and see her in the morning. With that settled she dozed off at last; it was almost daylight.

After breakfast on Sunday, before her resolution could falter, Alice phoned Nancy's house and spoke to Mrs. Warren.

"Who? Alice Marshall? Well she's in the General Hospital, my dear. Yes, her arm is broken, but apart from that she's all right. I'm sure she'd like to see you."

She can't know what I did or she wouldn't say that, Alice thought grimly. Travelling by bus, she made her slow way to the hospital, moving like a sleepwalker, her mind concentrated on the ordeal ahead. What to say? How to start? She opened Nancy's door and gazed in dumb misery at the girl who was sitting up in bed, her arm bulky in a cast.

Nancy looked up and a flush covered her pale face.

"Hello Alice," she said after a moment.

"I . . ."Alice began, and then stopped, not really knowing what to say. Her mind, usually so positive, was now a confused jumble of half thoughts and incomprehensible, vague feelings. "How are you, anyway?" she finally asked abruptly.

Nancy's flush faded, leaving her paler than ever.

"I'm okay."

Alice gripped the bottom rail of the hospital bed with both hands.

"I came to say," she tried afresh, "I mean, I didn't mean to . . . At least . . ." Stuck again, she stood with her mouth open, staring hopelessly. All at once the accumulated miseries boiled up inside her into a fierce rage — at Nancy for falling off, at Chips for being a yappy little pest, at life in general for putting her in this spot, but mostly fury at herself for causing the whole affair.

"Oh Catfish!" she shouted, stamped her foot, and collapsed into the chair beside the bed, where she burst into noisy tears.

Nancy stared, open-mouthed, amazed and appalled; but as the violent sobbing continued she timidly touched Alice's shoulder, and then more boldly put her whole good arm around the bowed figure.

"Alice don't . . . Please, Alice. You don't have to cry like that." Awkwardly she patted the shaking shoulders. "Oh gosh, for goodness' sake, you're making me cry, too." In fact, what with fatigue and pain, there were tears in her eyes, and soon both girls were weeping heartily together.

"This is . . . idiotic," Nancy said shakily.

"What are we . . . crying about?"

Alice raised a blotched, woeful face. "But Nancy, I might have *killed* you," she exclaimed.

Nancy gave a tentative, watery smile. "But you didn't. You might have knocked me down and broken my arm playing basketball or something just as easily."

"How can you be so . . . so forgiving? You should be absolutely furious." Alice wiped her eyes vehemently with the palms of her hands, and sniffed.

Nancy shook her head, dark hair swinging gently.

"Look, this may sound completely nuts, but I'm *glad* it happened. It made you come and talk to me, I mean really talk. I always liked you, and wished we could be friends."

A violent hiccuping sob rocked Alice.

"I've been so mean to you. You must despise me, the things I've done. Funny . . . I thought I *hated* you, but I guess I was just jealous."

"Jealous?" Nancy was honestly amazed. "Why on earth would you be jealous of me? You've got everything. You're pretty, and everybody likes you, and you can do so many things."

"I *was* jealous," Alice declared positively, "and it was simply because you can ride better than I can, and I couldn't stand being beaten at anything. I was so conceited," she continued, abasing herself as enthusiastically as she did everything else, "that I thought I had to be tops in every single thing. Also — it's queer, you know — once I'd started being horrible I couldn't seem to stop, though I often wanted to. Can you understand that?"

Nancy grinned, an engagingly impish grin which Alice had never seen. How could I? she thought. What has she ever had to grin about?

"Why are you laughing?" she asked.

"I was just thinking," Nancy replied, daring to tease, "that I bet you'll never be so humble again in all your life."

Alice's answering grin was disrupted by another convulsive hiccup. "I hope I never have to be."

She gazed dreamily into the distance for a moment, rubbing her cheeks where the drying tears had left sticky traces. "Have you ever had a sauna bath?" she asked.

"A couple of times, yes."

"You know how you sit there in the steam, looking at your arm, or your leg, and seeing the sweat come out in drops all over, and the drops run together and trickle down. Then after a while you go out and have a cold shower, or lukewarm if you're chicken, and afterwards you feel so clean and light, almost as though you could float. That's the way I feel now."

Nancy nodded. "I know. Purged."

"Purged, that's it. I'm purged of all the meanness and jealousy and general misery. Will we be friends, Nancy? And do things together?"

Nancy nodded vigorously, eyes sparkling.

"Oh, super. That'd be just great — to be one of the gang!"

"You'll be one of the gang, all right. They're simply not going to believe it when they see us walk up together. Can't you just see all those dropped jaws and popping eyes?" The girls giggled together.

"And you can come and school Misty over our jumps, and I'll go and ride with you and Gwen at John's stable." Nancy was glowing.

"This is going to be fun," Alice said gleefully.

She hiccuped again, caught Nancy's eye, and they both began to laugh.

Malabeam

by: Norma Joan Paul   *illustrations: Nick Poliwko*

Rivière Verte, Quisibis, Ste.-Anne, St.-Leonard, Bellefleur, Grand Falls. No, we were not on a train! My friend Sacobie and I were canoeing down the Saint John River in New Brunswick, the lovely homeland of the Maliseets.

I was glad when he suggested that we stop for a while. My muscles ached as we pulled the canoe up the grassy river bank. There was a comfortable place to sit where I could lean against one of the great dying elm trees that lined the shore.

I yawned and wished that I could coax a story from Sacobie. Then I remembered how we had stood in the morning sunshine near the power dam blocking the waters that had once roared over the Grand Falls. He had said something about "the Destroying Giant." That was the story I wanted to hear!

"What was it you called the falls this morning? *Checan . . . ? Checanek . . .?*" I began hopefully.

"*Che-ca-ne-ke-peag.*" My friend said the Maliseet word carefully. "The Destroying Giant."

I waited.

Sacobie stretched back on the grass under the old bare elm and, looking into the cloudless blue sky, began his story:

"There are several versions of this tale. I will tell you what was first told to me. In the olden times, perhaps more than five hundred years ago, the Indian village of Meductic was surrounded by a wooden palisade for, you see, the Maliseets lived in constant fear of attack by the Mohawks who lived far to the north. There was good reason for their fear. In the past the Mohawks had made surprise raids on the villagers, and hunting parties from Meductic going north in search of food or furs were always in

danger of capture by their great enemy.

"It was at the end of a peaceful summer when the fields of maize were green about the village of Meductic that the hunters ventured far up the river toward the north. They hunted in safety and most had returned to Meductic, but there remained on the distant hunting grounds an old man who was called by my name, Sacobie, with his daughter, Malabeam. The aged Sacobie moved more slowly than the young braves and he was just beginning to make ready to leave the Madawaska and return to Meductic.

"Malabeam was helping her father load the canoe when, without warning, a flint-tipped arrow flashed through the air and pierced the old man's breast. Malabeam fell to her knees beside her father but there was nothing she could do for him. Looking up, she found herself surrounded by a Mohawk war party. It was, perhaps, her beauty that saved her for after a few moments one of the Mohawks who could speak the Maliseet tongue promised to spare her life if she would lead the war party to Meductic. Indeed, if all went well, he promised that she would marry a Mohawk warrior.

"Malabeam looked out across the river where a great flotilla of canoes could now be seen. Five hundred warriors had come to destroy her people. She thought in despair of her relatives and friends resting peacefully at Meductic. What chance had they against so great a war party? In her heart there was a picture of the lovely river that lay between the Madawaska and Meductic. From that picture of the river came one terrible, secret thought that made the girl tremble from head to toe. Looking up with tears in her eyes, she promised to lead the Mohawks down the river to her people's village.

48

"When the last rays of light left the sky and the river became still and black, Malabeam was placed in the chief's canoe and the great party began the southward journey. Before long the canoes approached the falls at the mouth of the Madawaska. Malabeam warned the war party of the danger ahead and they portaged around the falls. The chief was pleased with Malabeam's behaviour and felt sure of reaching Meductic safely and destroying the Maliseets.

"Malabeam peered through the darkness at familiar places along the edge of the river. Many times she had passed this way as a little girl in the canoe of her father. She looked back at the war canoes and the weary Mohawks. They had travelled a long distance and the need for sleep weighed heavy upon their eyes.

"Quietly Malabeam suggested that they lash the canoes together in several long lines and thus they could sleep while floating down the tranquil river. The Mohawks did as she suggested and soon they slept while the canoes moved silently toward Meductic. Mile after mile they moved with hardly a sound. Then from the distance came the far-off roar of falling water. The sound grew louder, ever louder.

"When several of the warriors stirred and wondered at the sound, Malabeam assured them that it was the roaring of the falls on the Quisibis far to one side of them. The tired Mohawks did not notice that the water moved ever more swiftly. While the war party slept, Malabeam slipped unnoticed into the deep black river and, using every ounce of her strength, she managed to swim to shore.

"Too late the warriors awoke to the thundering sound of danger. Too late! In a rushing surge of water the canoes were swept over the edge of the great falls and into the whirlpools of *Checanekepeag*.

"Down the river from the great falls the little village of Meductic slept in peace. When Malabeam finally reached home, strong arms carried the exhausted girl to the wigwam of Sacobie. There, trembling, she told of the fate of the Mohawk war party. Soon, along the shore of the river, broken canoes and drowned warriors confirmed her story.

"Malabeam became the heroine of the Maliseets. No longer would they walk in fear of their ancient enemy. Even today the memory of the beautiful Malabeam, the princess of the river, remains dear to the hearts of her people."

Sacobie finished his story and we sat quietly, imagining that we could hear the distant sound of the falls. Or did we hear the echo of voices telling and retelling this story through the centuries? I wondered how many times this tale must have been told, over and over again. In the bitter chill of five hundred winters the legend of Malabeam was repeated to Maliseet boys and girls. Sacobie told the tale to me and now I pass it on to you. Remember the beautiful maiden of the river and someday you may tell her story as you sit around a campfire with your friends.

The Path

by: Sarah Coles   illustrations: Nick Poliwko

Although for many years friends have wondered at my reluctance to enter any woodland area, to walk along any wooded path, I have never explained this to anyone. After this long silence I feel I can no longer keep the secret, and so I am telling you. Perhaps, afterwards, I shall be able to live with peace of mind.

Many years ago our family had a summer cottage in the Canadian "bush." It was in a lonely stretch of dense woods and swamp, so I had to think up my own entertainment. I was used to this, being an only child. I would walk for half an hour in an easterly direction from our cottage until I came onto a path that could have been a pig run, except that there were no pigs around. I never wondered who had made the small, winding trail. It was there, so I thought, just for me.

The path wound among and over tree trunks, rocks and streams, and sometimes seemed to disappear altogether, but that was half the attraction. I was a small child, and able to duck under most branches and slip through most bushes without difficulty. I never came home without wet shoes and bruises and cuts when I walked along that path, and my parents berated or consoled me on different occasions, although it was more often the former than the latter. I was not to be turned away from the path's fascination. I went all day and every day, and always there seemed some new attraction.

I remember well the first time I stumbled upon it, while looking for wildflowers for the supper table. I ran along it with eager feet, gobbling up the miles and enchanted by the sights, until I realized how dark it was and turned for home. From that day forward, for many summers, that path caught my fancy and would not let me go.

Walking alone did not frighten me, but I remember at first feeling uneasy when I heard crackling sounds, the source of which, when I turned to see, would instantly fall silent. So I asked for a dog for my ninth birthday and every summer afterwards, until that one dreadful incident, an enormous brown and white Newfoundland trotted by my side. He was so huge and majestic that I called him King's Estate, and never shortened that name. I still heard the crackling sounds when I walked with him, but since he did not seem perturbed, I ignored them.

In the middle of my twelfth summer I saw an old Indian film at the dilapidated moviehouse in the nearest town. I was entranced, and that night, in bed, I had a marvellous idea — or so I thought. Not that my path had lost any of its charm, but I decided it would be even more fun if I played a game while I walked along it. I decided to pretend to be an Indian myself, with King's Estate as my faithful "sidekick."

I tried this the next morning, and it was even better than I'd guessed. King's Estate looked puzzled when I suddenly dropped flat on my stomach and pulled him down beside me, hissing, "Shh! Iroquois ahead!" But he soon caught the mood and bounded along barking beside me when I ran war whooping down the path, or slunk close to the ground whenever we were on the outskirts of an enemy camp. I heard more cracklings of twigs around me than ever before when I played this game, but I paid no attention. How I wish I had — now, so many years later!

Until I began to play the game I had never felt I had either the strength or the time to go right to the end of the path, if it had an end. I had also failed to notice that not a single trail led off it, as there would have been if the path had

50

been made by animals. Now, however, keeping my eyes mainly on the ground, tracking enemies who were usually just around the next bend, or behind that low clump of bushes, I couldn't help noticing this. There weren't even any trodden-down leaves, any broken underbrush. Surely, I thought, animals would leave a maze of tracks crisscrossing their main thoroughfare.

It never occurred to me that there might be no animals at all. There were always animals, weren't there? Especially in a woods without hunters? In a woods as deserted as these woods seemed to be?

Well, questions like these were soon forgotten as my game became more and more complicated and absorbing. I even went so far as to spend my worldly savings on an Indian costume from a craft store, and I made a headdress with a strip of deerskin and some feathers out of my large collection. I also stuck a bluejay's feather into the fur on King's Estate's massive head, a disguise to which he submitted peacefully, wearing the feather with a patient look.

Now that both of us looked the part, I played the game more intensely. I ran less, and stalked more. But I hardly ever uttered my prized and much-practiced war whoop now, because of

disturbing cries — more than echoes — that followed right after mine. But now that you know what the game was, let me describe it in more detail; it will take only a minute.

We would set off in the early morning, before my parents were awake, and stop at berry bushes for breakfast. We would continue until we came to a tall birch tree (B-B, I called it, having just read *1984*), where I would start the game. I would look around, and suddenly flop on a soft bed of moss, King's Estate beside me. After lying there for thirty seconds I would crawl along the ground until I reached a drop into a ravine that I called Devil's Pit. From there I could command a good view of the clearing in Devil's Pit where one of many enemy tribes had its camp. I would fit arrow after arrow into the bow which I had made (with considerable help from my father), and with deadly accuracy shoot down a few men who had strayed from the teepees.

The strange thing was that each time my arrow found its imaginary mark, I heard a sharp cry, which at the time I thought was the call of a bird. After this, the chief's child would discover the dead men and the whole tribe would be after me.

It was, I remember, during one of my desperate flights from them that King's Estate first showed signs of his later change. He ran ahead of me, and then stopped, whining, with fear in his voice and his eyes. But then he sped on with me again, until we reached my hideout, a hollow tree into which I could duck, and wait until the braves pounded past. Then we ran back home.

I *ran* home, rather than walked, because by this time my imagination would be almost uncontrollable, showing shadowy shapes flitting through the trees. I would barely take time to eat my lunch before dashing back as fast as I could to Devil's Pit, where the women and children had been left unguarded, and I would raid their camp, killing and stealing. Then back to my hideout to gloat over my deeds and wait until the hunting braves had returned past me in disgust. And then home again just in time for dinner.

As I said before, I had still never gone right to the end of my path, and so one day I packed a lunch and set off at sunrise, determined to see where it ended. The day was bright (I remember it vividly) and my spirits high. As soon as we struck the path, however, King's Estate, who was usually so good at staying by me, yelped as if he had been kicked, and shot off back home. I knew he would not come back, so I travelled on alone.

Feeling a little apprehensive — about

something that surely wasn't there — I began singing a song to keep my courage up. The song was one I had heard on the radio, but I changed the words into sounds to make it like an Indian chant. "*Boom* boom boom boom! *Boom* boom boom boom!" I sang when I came to the chorus, my favourite part. Suddenly I stopped. Was that an echo I heard, or an answering chant? It had come from the dank swamp to my right. Forcing my way to its mucky edge through thorn bushes and what looked like poison ivy, I peered through the gloom. I could see nothing; a dense mist had suddenly appeared, and soon I could not see my hand before my face.

I lay down where I was, waiting confidently for the mist to disperse as quickly as it had come. But it didn't. It got thicker — so thick I could almost touch it, and I became very cold. There was a nasty smell, too, coming from the swamp behind me. Then I heard twigs breaking, crackling as if underfoot, and bushes rustling. Someone or something was coming towards me! I froze.

The footsteps stopped so close beside me I didn't dare breathe, and there was a quick familiar sound, like the high note of a violin. An arrow leaving a bow! I ducked, and something brushed past my hair and thudded into the ground. I let out a squeak, and the footsteps moved away as if satisfied.

Almost at once the mist lifted. I saw that it was dusk. Surely not, I thought! It's only a couple of hours since I left home, not a whole day! I remembered the arrow, and searched where I thought it had struck. Nothing. I scrabbled among the nearby bushes. Nothing.

Suddenly a bird cried out. It was the last straw. In terror, I raced to the path, cannoned down it, ripped through the bushes, sobbing hysterically all the long way back, and wrenched open the door of our cottage, only to find it deserted. Looking wildly around, I spotted a note stuck to the cupboard above the stove. With increasing dismay I read, "Gone to town. Called you but you weren't around. See you."

Now the panic was rising. I noticed it was dark — very dark — outside. And there was a strange whimper coming from King's Estate's basket. I hurried over, only to see something unrecognizable there. That usually-shining, glossy coat was now burred and filthy-smelling from a deep cut in one shoulder. The flag tail drooped, the strong pads were cut and bruised. But worst of all were the eyes. Normally so contented and dark and trustful, they seemed now to be pure evil; out of reddish eyeballs there came a terrible look, a look that seemed to be of both the hunter and the hunted.

The most unearthly whining came out of its half-open mouth. I say "its" because although this creature *had* been King's Estate, here was no old and faithful friend. This was a *thing* that snarled and, breathing heavily, struggled to its feet. As it lurched towards me, I screamed and ran for the porch, slamming the

52

inner door. Unfortunately I had taught King's Estate, when he was a pup, how to open that door, and in seconds the horrible thing showed it had not forgotten. I ran outside. It followed, clumsily, and I managed to slip past into the cottage again, where I quickly locked the heavy oaken outer door. He — it — couldn't get through that, I hoped.

Inside, I locked all the doors and windows, pulled all the blinds and drew the curtains, and then sat down to calm my nerves.

Impossible! From outside came a sound I recognized, though only from old Jack London serials on TV. The sound of a wolf howl! When the first eerie wail stopped, another answered, and then a third right by the front door. Then I heard a snarling, spitting noise; the noise of combat. Lifting the corner of a curtain to look out, I could barely distinguish three grey forms grappling with a brown and white animal in the dim yard. Even though I could no longer feel that King's Estate was my dog, I was heartbroken when I saw that familiar shape go limp, and heard the others set up their howling again.

Then all the inside lights began to turn off and on, off and on. That was it!

I ran to the nearest door, burst it open and, heedless of the now-silent forms turning their glittering eyes towards me, ran for my life. I did not realize which way I was going until I felt the well-known path under my feet. On and on I went, past B-B, past all my scenes of combat and triumph, and was still running when I began to feel I was in unfamiliar territory. I had never gone this far before, so I slowed down. Then I heard the padding sounds close behind, and knew those deadly grey creatures were still after me.

I had never won any school prizes for speed, but now I ran like an Olympic medallist. On and on, never looking back or even sideways. After what seemed years, but was no more than minutes, I grew exhausted. I slowed, I stopped. Quiet. I listened. Ominous, total silence.

Suddenly the sky split open with a deafening clap of thunder and a brilliant flash of lightning that lit up a horrible scene. I was at the end of the path. In front of me was a clearing, and in that clearing was a shadowy camp. I caught a glimpse of translucent teepees and grey shapes before the rain cut down over them, leaving me in darkness. Then another flash of lightning lit up a group of men coming towards me. Or rather, what had once been men. They had dark hair and dark skins, but were unlike any living Indians. Terrible gaping mouths and hollow eye sockets, and long bloody spears in bony hands.

I screamed and fell on my face, but looked up upon another lightning flash. It was now a different scene. There was a huge battle going on, with bloodcurdling war whoops that sounded oddly familiar, until I realized that they seemed to be echoes of my own. Then another flash lit up a body-strewn place of death, with not a single living soul.

I heard the wind tearing at the branches, and suddenly I heard a long cry of despair close by me. Looking up, I saw a young Indian boy staring at the dead. He looked exactly like me.

* * * * * *

When I woke, I was in a hospital in a city a long way away from there. I have not been on that path, or on any path, in a woods since that day. My only reason for telling this story was that I would, having told it, be able to forget.

But it doesn't feel like that.

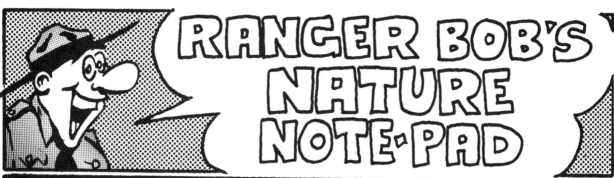

RANGER BOB'S NATURE NOTE-PAD

A SHY ANIMAL, AND RARELY SEEN, THE *CANADA LYNX* CAN BE FOUND COAST TO COAST IN MOST NORTHERLY REGIONS.

SOMETIMES WEIGHING AS MUCH AS 50 lbs., THE *CANADA LYNX* EATS ANYTHING HE CAN CATCH, INCLUDING FISH, TOADS, AND EVEN GRASSHOPPERS!

Did You Know:

RACCOONS OFTEN "WASH" THEIR FOOD BECAUSE THEY DO NOT HAVE SATISFACTORY SALIVA GLANDS!

©79 POLIWKO·THEOBALDS

STUDYNETS

MANY CENTURIES AGO IN THE HEART OF KOZAK UKRAINE STOOD A PEACEFUL VILLAGE CALLED GOOSE HOLLOW...

...PEACEFUL MOST OF THE TIME THAT IS...

YOU CABBAGE-HEAD! GET YOUR LAZY BUM OUT OF THIS HOUSE!!

...OUR CORPULENT HERO, IHOR IS HAVING DIFFICULTIES WITH HIS GENTLE WIFE, SONYA!

AS IHOR RECOUNTS HIS LATEST TRIALS TO HIS TRUSTING FRIEND, YURKO...

TO ARMS!! TO ARMS!! THE HETMAN * CALLS ALL KOZAKS TO JOIN HIM IN FIGHTING THE TURKS!!

YAHOO!! ANOTHER EXPEDITION!!

UH, YURKO WHO ARE THE TURKS?

THE TURKS, IHOR ARE A STRANGE FOLK WHO LIVE ACROSS THE BLACK SEA! THEY WEAR TURBANS, SMOKE FUNNY PIPES, AND MOST OF THEM HAVE MANY WIVES!

I WON'T GO!

WHY?

WELL IF EACH OF THEM HAS MANY WIVES THEN OBVIOUSLY THEY'RE MUCH MORE EXPERIENCED AT FIGHTING THAN WE ARE!!

* THE HETMAN WAS LEADER OF THE KOZAK ARMY.

NEXT DAY, TRAINING BEGINS IN EARNEST FOR THE UPCOMING CAMPAIGN...

KEEP MOVING!! YOU'RE SO OUT OF SHAPE THE VILLAGE EMBROIDERY CIRCLE WOULD GIVE YOU PROBLEMS!!

LATER AS IHOR AND YURKO RELAX...

HEAVENS, AM I EVER TIRED!

ME TOO IHOR! I HAVEN'T BEEN THIS TIRED SINCE THE LAST TIME I STOOD THROUGH THE ALL NIGHT EASTER MASS!!

CHERKAS 3 APRIL '79

YURKO?... JUST WHY ARE WE FIGHTING THE TURKS ANYWAY?!

IHOR, IT'S A MATTER OF POLITICS... ...THEY ATTACK AND PILLAGE OUR VILLAGES SO WE REPLY BY ATTACKING AND PILLAGING THEIRS!!

I DON'T SEE WHAT THAT HAS TO DO WITH POLITICS!

IT'S QUITE SIMPLE. IT DRAGS ON FOREVER, COSTS LOTS OF MONEY, AFFECTS EVERYONE AND MAKES NO LOGICAL SENSE—TO ME THAT'S POLITICS!

The Stained Glass Butterfly

BY DAVID HASKINS
ILLUSTRATED BY ROBIN BAIRD LEWIS

In a land far away where the midday sun is high in the sky and the light bounces off the white water into every shop window of the seafront town called Cluney Bay, there lived a glass cutter. He worked in his shop scoring the glass for picture frames and windows, street lamps and carriage lamps, but the town was so small he couldn't find enough business to keep him occupied.

At the end of the day his wife would say, "Is this all the money you have for me today, Thomas?"

"Yes, good wife," he would answer.

"Well you cannot expect me to put meat on the table and silks on my back with these few pennies," she nagged.

"But fish is cheap, and we're not planning any parties to dress up for," Thomas replied.

"Fish may be good enough for you," she argued, "but I won't put up with it. As for parties, who can we invite into this hovel? None of the people who matter in this town would come near the place."

"I matter," the glass cutter said softly.

One night, after his wife was in bed sound asleep, he got up quietly and stole upstairs to the garret. By the soft light of a candle he worked away at his favourite hobby, cutting and staining tiny figures made of glass and lead. At first he had made the lead too thick, and the glass broke under the strain of the lead filaments. Then he had coloured the glass too dark so that even the light of the midday sun would not pass through it. Then he had ground the glass too hard so that the polish was lost and the faces were pockmarked with holes. But with each new mistake he had learned how to correct the last one, until soon there were no more mistakes and his creations were nearly perfect.

He hung his stained glass figures in the window and sat down to imagine what beautiful colours they would shed into the room when the sun came up the next morning. There were designs in every colour, and shapes of seagulls and sheep and a jester and a lovely lady with a big floppy hat tied under her chin. But his favourite figure was a butterfly which he had stained a golden amber and made to look so lifelike that he half imagined it might flutter its wings and try to fly. Suddenly the candle flame dipped into the melted wax and snuffed itself out. Thomas knew it was time to creep back down the stairs to his bed before his wife awoke to discover him missing.

The next morning he could not keep his mind on his work for thinking how wonderful his butterfly must look, refracting the sun's beams through the small garret room. But work he did, filling orders for two large hall mirrors and three watchglasses. All through supper that night he kept looking at the clock, anxious for bedtime, and then the precious hour when he could sneak upstairs.

"I see by the books that you've been spending your time on those cheap watchglasses," his wife said at the table.

"Only three today," he said, "and they were all for gentlefolk. You'd be proud to know who came in the shop today: Mayor Findley's wife Janet, and Councillor Abraham Solstein himself, and if that weren't enough, old Joseph Pape the Miller's grandfather, spry as ever, walked down from the mansion with only a cane to help him, just to pick up his watch."

"Well why under the stars did you not charge them what they're willing to pay for your services, man! Are you not able to see good fortune when it's staring you in the face?" she accused.

"I charge what the job is worth, nothing less, nothing more," the glass cutter replied.

"Honestly, Thomas, I don't know how you expect me to get on, wasting away in this dreary hole. What a simpleton you are. You'll be lowering me into the ground in a pine box before my time, I fear."

"I doubt that, good wife," he said quietly.

Later, when he heard her reassuring snore from the far side of the bed, he lifted the covers and crept upstairs. He lit a new candle and hurried to the window. There was the butterfly, gently twisting about on the end of the fishing line that suspended it from a hook in the ceiling. Tom set the candle on the ledge below, and watched the light sparkle off the many facets of its wings. Then he moved the flame back and forth to better view the amber translucence of the glass. As he pulled the candle away, he accidently touched the left wing with the back of his hand. The butterfly flinched, momentarily closed its wings together, and then reopened them. Tom couldn't believe his eyes. The thing of glass and lead had moved! Impossible! Ever so softly he touched his fingers to the wing. Cold glass. He ran his thumb over the head. Cold lead. "A simpleton I am," he said to himself, and went back downstairs.

The next day was his wife's shopping day. "I've taken all the money I can find," she said as she left the shop. "Don't think you'll be dining off more than cornbread and beans on this paltry sum, Thomas."

As soon as she was safely down the road, Tom put his tools away and dashed upstairs. He had to see the butterfly in daylight.

When he got to the landing he hesitated, wondering for a moment what he would see. Slowly he turned the knob and peeked his head around the door. The whole room was awash with an orange amber glow. Sunbeams filtered through the butterfly's tiny wings into every corner, bouncing off the walls in golden streamers. Some hit the stained glass wings and reflected back through the window, flashing their intermittent light signals high into the sky. As chance would have it a glorious monarch, midway on its high flightpath south for the winter, spotted the radiant white dot far below. Something primitive compelled the creature to turn, something stronger than the migratory instinct, stronger than the threat of approaching winter storms, and he dove toward the light like iron drawn to a magnet. Two thousand feet down the live butterfly followed the beam to its source —

the glass butterfly — twisting about in the garret window.

Now Tom watched the monarch darting this way and that outside the window. He seemed dazed by the dazzling light and his great fall, his movements jerky as he crashed his body against the window, trying to break in. With every advance of the monarch against the glass, Tom thought he saw the amber butterfly recoil as though it too felt the shock.

"So you've found a friend, have you," Tom said to the model butterfly. "A handsome fellow too. But he won't last long if he carries on like that. His wings will tear, and then the trip south will be too much for him."

Tom unlocked the window and pushed it out on its hinge. The monarch flew past him unafraid, and, beating his wings in a show of delight, landed exactly on top of the glass imitation. There he spread out his black-veined wings, fully covering the amber glass, fluttered them a few times, and rested. Tom watched this little performance, marvelling at how the real butterfly completely masked the crafted one, how their two bodies seemed to blend together as one. As they turned, suspended by the fishing line in the sunlight, Tom saw that the underside of the glass butterfly showed the dark veining of the real one through its wings. The lead filaments which held the glass in place had become thin as human hair, and the leaden antennae sported a fuzz along them, and the leaden head was inset with two large eyes, and the leaden body was spotted with white dots. The butterfly and the lead and glass effigy were indistinguishable to Tom's eyes. He raised his hand to touch the orange wings, but stopped in midair for fear their bloom would rub off on his fingers.

Then the insect, seeing his open hand, swayed the nylon thread to and fro until it could reach Tom's fingertips. Carefully it grabbed hold with its six raspy legs and walked along his forefinger to his palm. Gone was the heavy weight of lead and glass! Tom lifted his hand to the window, slackening the line, to get a better look. The butterfly closed its wings upright, basking in the light. There was nothing underneath. Only this living monarch, settling comfortably on Tom's hand.

At that moment a balmy breeze blew in the open window. The butterfly, sensing the currents of the sky, fluttered briefly, lifted itself into the air, flew twice around Tom's head, and straight out the window. High up it soared, bobbing on the wind until it was only a pinprick in

Tom's sight, and then it was lost in the vast blue sky.

After a while Tom went back downstairs to his shop and took up the diamond cutter again. He cut a window for George Stowbridge, and a mirror for Lady Montmorency. The window was so large and so clear that Mr. Stowbridge almost walked through it when he came to pick it up. The mirror gave so true a reflection of Lady Montmorency's ageing countenance that she refused to pay for it, and told her chauffeur as she went out the door to smash it at Tom's feet. Tom broke a wine bottle he had in the waste bin and gave the mirror to the chauffeur instead.

Tom's wife was furious when she heard about the mirror. He expected she would be. She ranted and raved about the price of a dress, a simple dress to wear on Sundays, the price of a weekend on the town, the price of entertaining the Elton-Danby's for dinner, the price of a new carpet for the front parlour, and the price of a hairdresser to give her a new coiffure.

Tom listened patiently. When she finished, he said, "Do you think we'd be happier if we had a child, good wife?"

"A child is it! You'd like that wouldn't you. Me suffering a young'un into this house, running after it, feeding it and changing it I suppose until I was blue in the face. Well if you think that is going to keep me satisfied with your few pennies for my comfort, you've got another think coming to you."

"No, I don't suppose it would make much of a difference," said Tom.

That night, when he heard his wife snoring, he stole up to the garret, opened the window, and gazed out at the midnight sky. A wisp of a cloud swept across in front of the full moon. It looked like the mane of a wild stallion. On the breath of the night wind, Tom thought he heard a horse neighing afar off.

He went to his bench and lit another candle. His next project of glass and lead, he decided, would be a winged horse. And it would be life size.

The Echo Princess

by: Marina McDougall   *illustrations: Barbara Eidlitz*

Long ago, when mountains were made out of glass and fairies and people lived together in harmony, there was a fairy king who had three daughters. They lived in an enchanted palace by a lake. The two older sisters grew up to be beautiful fairies and soon they were married and settled in palaces of their own. But the youngest fairy princess, Tihany, the loveliest of the three with her golden hair and deep violet eyes, stayed at home. She had no voice and she could not speak.

Every morning she herded her father's golden-haired goats out to the emerald green pasture and every evening she led them to the sapphire lake. While the goats drank, she sat on her favourite pink quartz rock and gazed at the water, admiring her own reflection. Her face was as lovely as the sunset, but — sad to say — her heart was as hard as a diamond.

One evening, as she smiled and made pretty faces at herself in her lake-mirror, the water trembled until she could no longer see her reflection. Her face puckered into a frown as a bearded head wearing a crown emerged from the water.

"I am the King of the Waters," said the apparition. "Please, Tihany, fill this silver bucket with milk from your enchanted goats. My son, Balaton, is very ill and nothing can cure him except the milk of golden-haired goats."

Tihany shook her head impatiently. She wanted the King to go away so she could go on admiring herself.

"If my son cannot have the goat's milk by tonight, he will die," said the King of the Waters. "I beg you, Tihany," added the old King, bowing his white head before the heartless princess.

But Tihany only shook her head again, this time stamping her pretty foot.

"Then I will make a bargain with you," said the King in a hard voice. "If you milk the goats for me, I will give you your voice back."

When she heard that, Tihany smiled her most beautiful smile and jumped to her feet. She took the silver bucket, filled it in the blink of an eye with enchanted goat's milk, and handed it to the King of the Waters with a pretty curtsey. As he took the bucket from her, the King lifted a goldfish out of the lake and gave it to Tihany.

"Swallow this," he commanded. Then he sprinkled magic seaweed and pearls on Tihany's golden hair and said, "When you feel the goldfish tickling your throat you will be able to speak." Then he turned and rode away on the crest of three gigantic waves towards the middle of the lake.

When Tihany could no longer see the King of the Waters in the distance, she felt a little tickle in her throat. She took a deep breath, opened her mouth and out came the most beautiful tinkling voice that anyone has ever heard.

Every evening from that day on Tihany sang beautiful songs to her reflection, while sitting on the pink quartz rock. Her sweet voice travelled along the water and soon everyone who lived by the lake came out in the evenings to listen to her singing. Her fame spread and people came from far and wide to hear her.

Young Prince Balaton rose to the surface of the lake every evening to listen to her. His eyes grew dreamier each day.

"You would be foolish to fall in love with Tihany, my son," warned the King of the Waters, gravely shaking his head. "She has a face as beautiful as the sunset and a voice as sweet as a nightingale's, but her heart is made of hard diamond. She will not return your love."

But young Prince Balaton had already lost his heart.

"Sing me a song, Tihany," he would

plead. "Sing to me about love."

"I sing for no one except myself," replied Tihany. Then she added with a laugh, "But I will sing you anything you please if you bring me a gift. Bring me a giant conch full of pearls."

Prince Balaton descended to his underwater palace of seaweed, pearl shells and foam. He filled a smooth pink conch with pearls and swam to the pink quartz rock. Then he placed his offering at Tihany's feet and looked up at her. She smiled at him over the pearls and started to sing a sweet love song. Balaton brought her a gift of pearls every day after that just so he could listen to her sing in her beautiful voice about how much she loved him. After a while he almost came to believe the words of the song, forgetting that he had paid for them.

The young prince was not the only

customer.

"Sing us a lullaby, Tihany," asked the little elves who worked in the vineyards of Badacsony, the Wine Mountain.

"You know my price," smiled Tihany. "Bring me a basket of amethysts. Then you will have your lullaby."

The priest from the nearby village went to see her one day.

"With a voice as beautiful as that," he said, "you should praise God."

"If God wants me to sing his praises," answered the selfish princess, "let him send me a dress embroidered with diamond droplets and angel's hair."

And so Tihany continued to live for herself, smile at herself, and sing to herself only. The days passed. Then one evening Prince Balaton did not appear with his gift. Instead, Tihany saw the old King of the Waters come hurtling towards her on the crest of three gigantic waves.

"My son Balaton is ill," he said. "He will not live very long. Sing into this magic box, Tihany, so I can take your song down to his bedside."

"But where are your treasures?" Tihany asked. "You know that I only sing for payment!"

"My son has already brought you all my treasure," the King thundered, "and we have nothing more to give. Balaton is dying of a broken heart because of you. He loves you but he knows he cannot hear you sing again because he has nothing left to bring you as a gift."

Tihany shook her head. "If you do not pay me, I will not sing. Why should I waste a song on someone who is so poor that he has nothing to give me?"

"Have you forgotten how powerful I am?" shouted the King of the Waters, trembling with anger. "Have you forgotten how you got your lovely voice?"

"No, I haven't forgotten," answered Tihany. "You gave me my voice to save your son. But now I have all your treasure as well." She looked into the sad eyes of the old King and said with a cold smile, "Without your treasures you are nothing." Then, turning on her heels, she went back to her golden goats.

The King of the Waters disappeared in the angry green waves and a terrible storm raged over the lake for three days and three nights. On the fourth morning the waters were a calm blue once more. There was not even a ripple on the smooth surface.

"Prince Balaton is dead," whispered the goldfish to the seagulls.

"Prince Balaton is dead," whispered the gulls to the elves.

Soon everyone heard the sad news and everyone mourned for the handsome young prince. People shook their heads at Tihany and no one asked her to sing again. The King of the Waters buried his son in the heart of the Wine

Mountain, and the elves, to show their sorrow, molded the whole mountain into the shape of a coffin.

Then the powerful King of the Waters turned his anger into a terrible revenge. Where the lake had been as smooth as a mirror before, it was now constantly raging with storm and there was not a moment's lull when someone could look into the water and see his own reflection. One evening, when Tihany brought her goats to the water, an enormous wave swept the whole herd into the lake until the last golden goat was sucked down to the bottom of a boiling whirlpool.

Tihany, terrified, ran into the nearest cave to escape the angry King of the Waters. But he followed her and rolled a huge stone into the mouth of the cave so that the entrance was completely sealed off from the outside world. With a last pounding of his fists, he uttered this terrible curse:

"I have always kept my word and what I have given you I will not take back. But, in punishment for your selfish greed, you will live in this cave forever and, if anyone should ever speak to you, you will repeat every word seven times!"

The glass mountains have turned into the green hills since then and fairies no longer inhabit the earth. But if you visit Lake Balaton in Hungary you will still find goat-hoof pebbles on the lakeshore after a storm. Those are the hooves of the golden goats, turned to stone. Mount Badacsony has kept the shape of a coffin to this day and its slopes are still covered with vineyards. And, if you wander through the forests of Tihany, you will find a certain spot where you can stand and shout anything you please and an echo will faithfully repeat your words — exactly seven times — before they dissolve in the sad murmur of the foaming waves.

My Cat Likes Milk

by: Nancy Prasad
illustration: Nancy Lou Reynolds

My cat likes milk,
   And so do I.

My cat likes eggs,
   And so do I.

My cat likes porridge,
   And so do I . . .

We always eat breakfast together.

My cat eats cheese
   And asks for more.

My cat eats bacon
   And licks his whiskers.

He eats ice cream
   And purrs louder . . .

We always eat lunch together.

But, my cat likes fish
   That isn't cooked.

He eats liver
   And kidney and heart.

He hunts frogs
   And mice and birds . . .

We separate for supper.

Yoga Is For You

by: Belva Kalbfleisch   illustrations: Susan Cook
photos: NFB Photothèque, Jack Cockburn

What is over five thousand years old but as new as today? That someone as young as two years and as old as ninety-nine can enjoy? That will strengthen your spine, improve your lung power and keep your muscles elastic and firm? That had its beginnings in the Eastern Hemisphere but is fast gaining popularity in the West, including Canada?

The answer is a four-letter word — *yoga.*

You are never too old to start a daily program of yoga, but the earlier you begin, the better chance you have of enjoying your life to its fullest.

When yoga is mentioned, many people think of magic. Or they connect it with snake charming, fire swallowing, or walking painlessly on a bed of sharp nails. Some people think it is fortune telling, hypnotism or even talking to the spirits of our ancestors! Yoga is none of these.

Yoga is a practice which will help you improve physically, making your body healthier and stronger. It will improve your mental outlook, help you to remain cool and collected in times of stress, and enable you to develop spiritually, exploiting all your latent powers.

The word "yoga" means to *join* or *unite.* That means you will be using your body, your mind and your spirit all to the fullest. The goal is *hatha yoga,* or *physical well-being.* The different body positions which you learn to make a part of your daily life are called *asanas.* Some of them are planned from watching the way animals move, and are named after the appropriate creatures.

Yoga is different from calisthenics; you follow the needs of your own body, and stop when you have reached your own limit. You do not strive for the goals of others. Every body is different, every need is different. With daily practise, you will find that your performance of asanas is easier, and that you are able to do things which once you thought impossible. Exercise should and can be a happy time, when you get to know and like yourself better. Encourage your family to join you on the floor. Help your parents and grandparents to live every day of their lives to its fullest.

Pranayama, or *breath control*

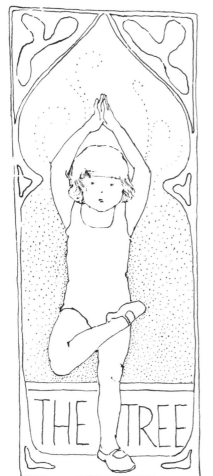

TRIPOD HEADSTAND

THE TREE

teaches us to use the full extent of our lungs. Most people use about one-fifth of their lungs with shallow breathing. Yet *prana (life force)* is free. All we need to do is learn to draw it in, filling the bottom of our lungs, the middle and the top. Did you know that you can live without solid food for more than a month, and survive without sleep or even liquids for a week? But without air to breathe, you would die in minutes.

Here are a few ways of improving your breathing, followed by directions for performing several asanas. Once you become enthusiastic, get a book with pictures and easy-to-follow directions for you and your family. A good one is *Yoga For Children,* by Kareen Zebroff.

BREATHING

COMPLETE BREATH

Sit in a comfortable position on the floor or a firm chair. Don't slump. Keep your thorax straight to make it easier to fill your lungs. Inhale slowly, through the nose, expanding your rib cage by pushing out the abdomen to fill the bottom of the lungs. As you continue to breathe in slowly, the tummy will come in a bit as the middle and top of your pear-shaped lungs fill.

Drop the chin to lock the breath in, for five seconds. Raise the chin and exhale slowly, through the nostrils, pulling the tummy in to push every bit of stale air out. Repeat the inhaling and exhaling three or four times. It is a nice sensation to close your eyes while practising this breath. It will build up resistance to respiratory infections, make you feel more alert, able to think better, and will relieve tension when you are facing school tests and assignments.

COOLING BREATH

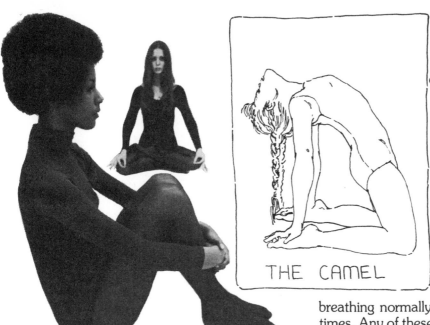

THE CAMEL

When you have better posture, you will have more energy. Get on your knees with toes pointed back, and legs together. With hands on waist, bend your head and body slowly backward as you push your pelvis forward. As you advance, let one hand hang down, placing the palm on the sole of the foot, and the other hand on the other foot. Pinch the buttocks together, pushing thighs and pelvis forward so you get a good steady stretch, breathing normally. Don't do it more than three times. Any of these asanas need be practised only once or twice for maximum benefit. When you have mastered the camel, move on to the
PELVIC STRETCH

Kneel, sitting back on your heels. Place your hands one at a time flat on the floor behind you with your arms straight down from the shoulders. Letting your head hang back, push up on the pelvis, raising your hips off the feet and legs. Hold for five seconds. Lower yourself and come forward to relax in the
CURLING LEAF or POSE OF THE CHILD.

Kneel with buttocks on heels, the top

THE CAT

THE PLOUGH

This is important for reducing fever because it cools the body. It will decrease the appetite if you have a few pounds to lose. It is also helpful in avoiding colds because it purifies the bloodstream.

Sitting in a comfortable position, make a trough of your tongue between open lips. Inhale through this trough slowly, making a hissing sound like a snake. Exhale slowly through the nose. Repeat several times.

ASANAS

As a practioner of yoga, you should sit on the floor as much as possible. Sit with legs crossed and drawn close to the body. Tailors in India have sat this way while working for years, and are known to be free of kidney and pelvic area problems.

STORK

Balance is important to our well being. Stand firmly, preferably in bare feet and not on a mat. Put arms out at shoulder level. Plant one foot against the calf of the other leg. Flap arms as if flying. You can hop around on one foot when your balance is good. Change legs.

CAMEL

The camel is gentle enough for grandparents but beneficial to all ages because it will correct round shoulders and hunched backs.

of your hands on the floor beside your heels. Slowly lower the head to the floor with your chest against your thighs. Shut your eyes and relax. This is good for improving complexion because it brings a fresh flow of blood to your head and face. You should relax in this pose after every asana.

ROCK AND ROLL

For all ages. It massages the spine, where the central nervous system is housed. It is a good warm-up and energizer. Sit on the floor with your knees bent, hands clasped under them. Put your head on your knees so that the spine is rounded. Keep head tucked on knees throughout. Rock gently back as far as you can, massaging every vertebrae. Make the rocking as gentle as an empty rocking chair in a breeze.

PLOUGH

Important because it massages the liver, spleen and kidneys, and makes the abdominal muscles stronger. Lie on back on rug, hands by your sides. Raise legs slowly. Push down with fingers on floor to raise the hips. Don't bounce; make it a smooth motion. Try to put your toes to the floor over your head, hands and arms stretched out at sides. At first you may feel smothered, so don't stay in it very long, but do come out of it smoothly, letting your legs down slowly to the floor. You can do a number of things when you master the plough, such as bringing the knees down by the ears. When you advance, try putting the hands near the shoulders, fingers toward body, and push over into a backward roll. Be careful. Remember you only do what *your* body can do.

LION

Do the lion to improve your voice, and to ease a sore throat. It is a lot of fun! Sit on heels, toes on floor, hands on thighs. Slide fingers down thighs until they are on the floor, spread out with hands flat. Raise body off heels, come forward, opening eyes wide and sticking your tongue out as far as it will go. Now roar like a lion! Sit back, relax, and repeat three times.

WHEEL

Stand a short distance from a wall with your back towards it. Put hands on wall and gradually walk down it. When the hands reach the floor, you are in a wheel. Get someone to support your back the first time you try this.

SPONGE or RAG DOLL

A very important way to help you learn to relax. Lie flat on mat, feet slightly apart. Each muscle in turn is tensed, then relaxed, from the feet to the head, including the muscles of the face.

Yoga has several branches of learning, some of which require years of devotion and deep study before the student can practice them. *Yogi* is the name given to a person who has mastered the art of yoga. Patanjali, who lived in India about 200 B.C., was the first to write about it. Before that time, yoga had been handed down from master or *guru* to pupil. Patanjali is known as the "Father of Yoga."

Start today to make the rest of your life fuller and healthier by daily practice of the old yet ever new life-giver — yoga.

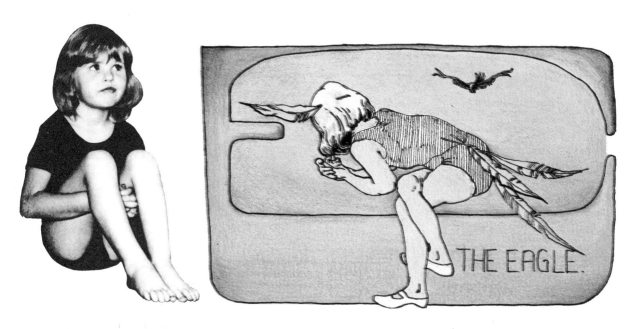

THE EAGLE.

SKY PUPPETS

by: Jannis Hare
illustration: Robin Lewis

The kite he made an hour ago
now drifts and glides; a bird on wing
above the trees. Yet down below
it is a child who holds the string.

The craft is cradled on the wind.
A dancing colour in the sun
it draws young thought beyond the earth
to where his dreams have just begun.

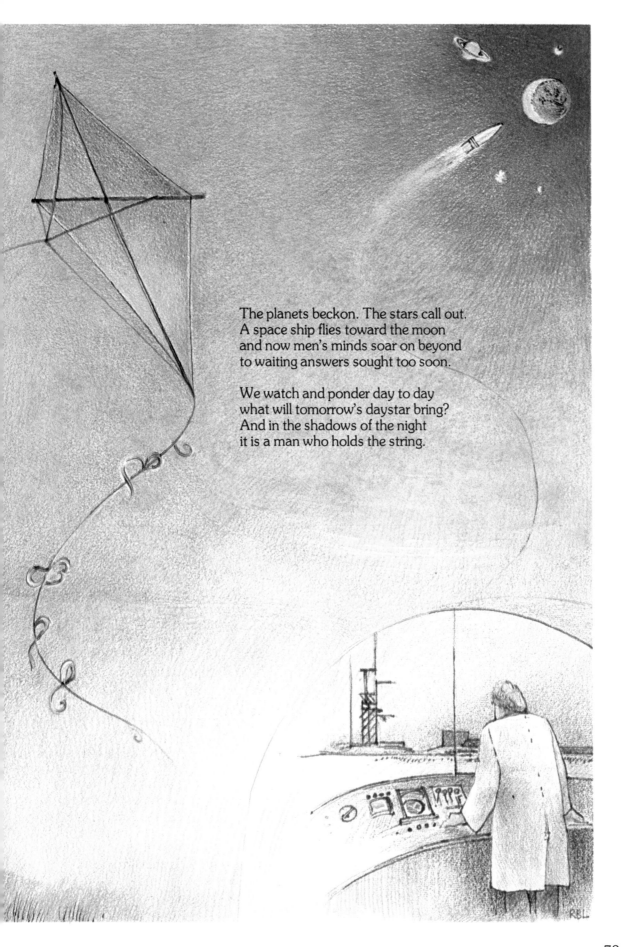

The planets beckon. The stars call out.
A space ship flies toward the moon
and now men's minds soar on beyond
to waiting answers sought too soon.

We watch and ponder day to day
what will tomorrow's daystar bring?
And in the shadows of the night
it is a man who holds the string.

A Canadian Cave Bestiary

by: M.B. Fenton,
Department of Biology, Carleton University

To many people thoughts of caves are filled with visions of swooping bats, explorers following a guiding string as they try to trace their way out, and exciting possibilities of hidden treasure. As an animal that orients by vision, a man without a light in a cave is like a fish out of water, and yet to many animals caves are home. Some cave dwellers, known as *troglobites,* only occur in caves and are specialized enough to spend their entire lives underground.

Many different groups of animals include troglobitic species. There are cave *flatworms* and *earthworms, beetles* and *scorpions,* and *fish* and *salamanders* to mention only a few. Most obligatory cave dwellers lack pigment, meaning that their bodies are white or cream-coloured, superficially resembling albinos. Troglobites are usually blind and rely on their senses of smell, touch, and vibration to locate food and mates or to gather information about their environment. Most troglobitic insects have lost the ability to fly and the limbs of cave dwellers tend to be longer and more slender than those of surface relatives.

To date one *isopod* species from Alberta is the only Canadian troglobite. The dearth of troglobites in Canada is related to the time that the caves have been available for coloni-

zation by animals. The Pleistocene glaciers only retreated from most of Canada about 12,000 years ago, and in North America most troglobitic species occur south of the limit of glaciation.

Canadian caves are occupied by animals, but they are not the specialists (troglobites) that occur in caves elsewhere.

Caves offer mixed blessings to their inhabitants, and one of the most important drawbacks is energy. Life on our planet runs on sunlight which is converted by green plants to chemical energy by *photosynthesis,* the basis of primary productivity. Visitors to caves will have noted that they are dark — pitch black — and no sunlight means no primary production. Therefore animals spending their entire lives in caves cannot be herbivores.

In Canada spiders that live in caves eat insects such as fungus gnats, which also live in caves, and insects such as mayflies, that emerge from streams flowing through caves. Troglobites such as the cave fish called *Typlichthyes* from Kentucky must be highly specialized to find their food. These fish often hunt isopods, small crustaceans that swim by vibrating their many legs. The cave fish locate the isopods by listening for these vibrations, relying on specialized cells called *neuromasts* to detect

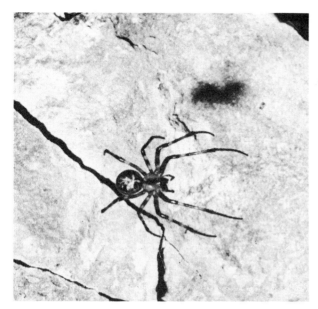 

the swimming prey.

Many other troglobites and a host of less specialized cave dwellers exploit less savoury food. Although it seems indelicate to our palates, many cave organisms feed on *detritus,* a mixture of dung, dead animals and dead plants.

Biologists know of no mammals or birds that are troglobites, and explain this by energy budgets. Since birds and mammals are warm blooded, they require considerable energy to survive (stay warm) and the food in caves is not high in calories. In Canada pack rats and some other rodents such as deer mice and white-footed mice live in caves, using them as places to spend the day, venturing forth at night to gather their food. You might ask why, if the food in caves is not rich enough for the energy requirements of warm blooded animals, would some species bother to live there? There are at least two reasons, temperature and predators.

Caves are usually pleasantly cool on hot summer days and rather warm in winter. Indeed, recording thermometers left in caves have shown that their temperatures are more or less the same in summer and in winter, in some areas between 1° and 10°C. For a deer mouse, living in a cave means that in midwinter in eastern Ontario the temperature outside its cave nest may be 5°C while a comparable temperature for a neighbour living outside is -20°C. Many mammals, from mice to porcupines and bears, find a favourable retreat in caves in winter because of their relative warmth.

In Canada, the winter temperature conditions in caves are crucial to the survival of our bats. As consumers of insects, Canadian bats are faced with an almost total absence of food in winter and while some species migrate to avoid winter, most hibernate, usually in caves. The body temperature of a hibernating bat is the same as that of the cave environment, often from 1° to 5°C.

Canadian bats do not occupy caves in summer. The stable temperatures that make them excellent for hibernation render them unsuitable in summer, when bats move to other roosts, often in buildings, where the temperatures range from 25° to 40°C. Bats start to return to caves in August when they are seeking mates and places to hibernate. Caves fulfill two vital functions in the lives of many Canadian bats, providing them with sites for mating and for hibernation.

Caves offer some protection against predators which rely on vision to find their prey. Birds such as the oilbirds of South America, or the swiftlets of Southeast Asia nest in caves and avoid many predators that would feed on their young. The swiftlets are well known to man as the source of bird's-nest soup. Bats too find caves relatively safe places to spend the day, out of reach of many potential dangers — but not all bats live in caves.

For me one of the greatest treasures of caves is *echolocation,* the means of orientation in total darkness used by oilbirds, most bats, and some swiftlets. Echolocation involves the production of sounds and listening for the echoes of these sounds that rebound from objects in the animal's path. The bats of Canada also use their echolocation to find their insect prey, but that's another story . . .

Dick Mallet

AN EPIC IN CRIME DRAMA

"I HAD BEEN WITH INSPECTOR HENDERSON IN HIS OFFICE WHEN THE CALL CAME IN. AMOS THORNHURST HAD JUST BEEN FOUND DEAD IN HIS STUDY—AN APPARENT SUICIDE! SINCE IT WAS A SLOW NIGHT, I DECIDED TO TAG ALONG... I'D NEVER SEEN A MILLIONAIRE BEFORE..."

...ESPECIALLY A DEAD ONE!!

MIGHTY BIG HOUSE!

HEY, MALLET, WAIT A MINUTE, EH?!

...INSPECTOR HENDERSON OF THE POLICE—AND THIS IS DICK MALLET!

WHERE'S THE STIFF?

RIGHT THIS WAY SIR.

"I COULD TELL RIGHT OFF THAT NOBODY REALLY CARED THAT AMOS THORNHURST WAS DEAD! THERE WASN'T A RED EYE IN THE ROOM WHICH MEANT THAT NOT A SINGLE TEAR HAD BEEN SHED OVER THE DEAD TYCOON..."

BENSON, THE BUTLER

ANDREW THORNHURST, AMOS' SON

ANNETTE, THE MAID.

THE DEAD MAN.

JOSH, AMOS' NEPHEW

77

78

M. CHERKAS 1979

RANGER BOB'S NATURE NOTE-PAD

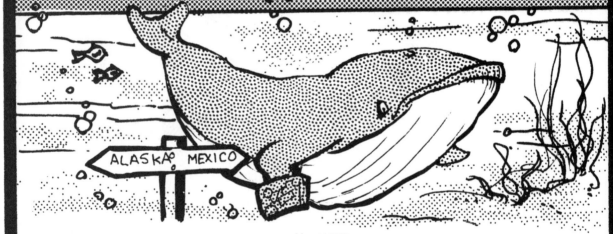

Did You Know:

~THAT THE *DOUGLAS FIR* TREE CAN HAVE A LIFE-SPAN OF *OVER 1,000 YEARS!*

ALASKA   MEXICO

EACH YEAR, OVER 11,000 CALIFORNIA GREY WHALES MAKE AN ASTOUNDING 6000-MILE TREK BETWEEN FEEDING GROUNDS IN THE ARCTIC'S BERING SEA AND THEIR BREEDING GROUNDS IN SUNNY MEXICO: *THE LONGEST KNOWN MIGRATION OF ANY MAMMAL!*

Wolverine

by: Mary Daem   illustrations: Barbara Eidlitz

"Gosh I'm lucky!" The wind caught Arnie's yellow hair and swirled it around his face.

The helicopter which had brought the boy and his uncle to the slab of flower-filled meadow high on Boulder Mountain diminished to bee-size in the distance.

The ride above sharp peaks and hidden lakes and waterfalls had thrilled the twelve-year-old. And ahead lay a whole summer with his Uncle Bill, working the Crazy Creek claims. Arnie took a deep breath of the clear mountain air and tried not to shiver as a cold gust blew around him.

"Time to move!" he heard his uncle say. "Can't stay here or the bears will get us."

Arnie looked over his shoulder. With Uncle Bill he never quite knew when he was being teased.

"Saw about fifty bears here once," his uncle added, and winked.

When Arnie picked up his pack it felt as if a whole mountain was in it. His uncle was already moving towards the thick scrub of trees that bordered the meadow, walking as if his much bigger pack contained only air. Arnie hurried.

A faint trail led upward through the trees. It skirted towering cliffs of granite. Before he had gone a hundred yards Arnie's muscles screamed at him to stop. Perspiration ran from his hairline; his lungs ached.

When his uncle called a rest at the edge of a rock slide Arnie collapsed as if a loose boulder had bounced off his head. This was going to be fun? He shut his eyes and groaned silently.

The smell of his uncle's pipe drifted towards him. A shadow floated across his hot face and marmots whistled their shrill alarm as the eagle threatened them. Arnie brushed hungry mosquitoes away and gradually his breathing eased. Perhaps he might live after all! He opened his eyes to see.

From a large crevice between two grey rocks an animal looked out. Arnie could see the eyes that gleamed like fire. The head was

81

brown and wedge-shaped. Slowly the lips lifted in a snarl. Arnie shivered. He was afraid.

"You devil!" exclaimed his uncle, seeing the wolverine at the same time. "If he decides to follow us we may as well call it quits. I mind one time a wolverine got into a cabin I had and tore it apart. He's the only animal I know that kills for revenge. He's the only animal I hate!" He knocked the ashes from his pipe and stood up.

The evil face vanished into the rocks.

Arnie thought about the wolverine as the trail grew fainter and more difficult. Twice he looked back, but he could see nothing. That didn't stop him fancying a wolverine behind every tree.

And now it was rocks they clambered over; Arnie felt clumsy when he let a loose one roll beneath his feet. His uncle scrambled across them like a marmot.

At the brim of a deep gorge they stopped and looked over the edge and down to the narrow twisted thread of Crazy Creek, rushing and fighting downwards. Arnie could just see the white froth, and the jagged rocks that stuck up through it.

His uncle took out his pipe again; using the stem of it to point, he showed his nephew the low grey cabin built on the flat point of land well above the broiling creek. "That's it," he grunted, with rough pride in his voice.

"Wow!" was all Arnie found to say. How was he expected to get down there?

But inch by inch he cautiously followed, more afraid to be left behind than to go ahead. His foot slipped; a hail of loose rock dislodged and went flipping into the canyon. Arnie's stomach clenched.

"Well, there she is!" Arnie could hardly hear his uncle over the roar of the creek.

Pulling off his pack with a great sigh of relief, Arnie tried to look delighted. But he was wondering how two people could live in such a small cabin for a whole summer.

Arnie was so tired that he fell asleep on the narrow bunk in the warm cabin before he had half finished his supper. The sound of dry wood crackling in the stove was the last thing he heard. And though he slept well, his sleep was filled with grizzly bears and wolverines and rocks, rocks, rocks.

The smell of bacon frying woke him. He was starved. His uncle laughed at him the way he attacked the food.

After breakfast they descended to Crazy Creek. Glacier born, it was cold, and the air in the canyon bottom was a match for it. Arnie was glad of his thick woolen shirt.

Before he had gone out to civilization the previous fall, Arnie's uncle had set up rough wooden boxes with slats across them to catch any fine gravel that might wash down the creek. Hopefully the gravel would contain flaked gold and small nuggets from the edge of some ore body above them. Uncle Bill showed Arnie how to lean down and pick out the rougher gravel that was caught, and toss it out. The finer gold and sand would be caught in the wooden riffles, or cross bars, and held. When there was a good build-up, Arnie and his uncle would divert the creek just enough to let them remove the riffles and collect the residue, place it in an old tub and carefully pan it again. When the pan was swished around and around, the lighter material floated off and the heavier gold remained.

Arnie found it backbreaking work. In the cold water his fingers stiffened. But he forgot all that in the excitement of seeing for himself the glint of a nugget — the size of a pinhead, but real gold!

The days were not all work. There was fishing. With the sun inching down the rocky sides of the gorge Arnie fished for the small trout with silver speckled sides. The fish were fun to catch, and fried in cornmeal, crisp and hot, they were delicious.

But one day Arnie lost the catch he had tossed on the bare rock behind him. A mink was racing away with the last fish before Arnie turned around. At first he was cross, but then he saw the funny side. Fishing again, he tossed his prize far back of him.

"One for you, Mr. Mink," he laughed.

But even above the sound of running water he heard the snarl. Crouched above the bounty was a wolverine. His squat, bear-like body was hunched possessively, and his short bushy tail stuck straight up. The sharp teeth and evil eyes defied the world.

Arnie didn't argue. And after that, when they left the cabin to wander out of the gorge and across the mountains in search of the main vein of gold-bearing rock Uncle Bill was certain he could find, they made sure that the door of the cabin was locked with a heavy bar and the windows shuttered.

Arnie grew tanned and tough. His packs were as light as a feather.

Near the end of summer his uncle asked Arnie's help in removing a huge boulder that had lodged sometime past in the middle of Crazy Creek near the cabin.

"If we could just figure out some way to get that fellow moved and set our sluice box

just right, we could catch a lot of the heavy stuff that's settled behind it. Two of us ought to be able to do it if we set our minds to it. You work well, Arnie."

Arnie's face warmed beneath its tan. His uncle had been careful with praise.

The job was more than they had expected. They used poles and shovels, and stood knee-deep in the icy water. Soaked, they heaved and pushed in vain.

"Set that pole right there," Uncle Bill snapped. When you hear me say 'SO!' throw your weight behind it. No old rock is going to get the best of me."

Over the swoosh of water, Arnie's sharp ears heard something. He looked up — just in time to see the hunched squat body of the wolverine crouched on an overhang, ready to pounce on his uncle's bent back.

"Watch out!" the boy shouted, loosening his grip on the pole. It snapped back with a chilling crack, and Arnie's uncle lay face down in the cold waters of Crazy Creek, drowning.

Arnie could never tell how he found the strength to pull his uncle from the creek, turn him over, and breath for him until he could do it for himself. He was a heavy man. His head was cut and one leg hung limply, badly crushed.

The journey to the cabin was a struggling crawl. When Arnie got him to his bunk and removed his wet clothes, the boy's stomach turned over. Bare bone showed on the crooked leg. And the gash on his uncle's forehead gaped wide. He would do his best, but without help his Uncle Bill would die.

Through the long night Arnie worked to keep him warm. He thought of the sharp peaks they had flown over so easily, and he thought of the creeks and ravines to be crossed. Arnie was desperately afraid. In seven days the helicopter was due to pick them up, but looking down at his uncle lying so quietly on the narrow bunk, Arnie knew that he couldn't wait.

He filled the cabin with wood, left food and water within his uncle's reach, fastened shut the windows, and barred the door from outside. His uncle, lying so helpless in the dim cabin, would be defenseless against the devil wolverine if he chose to claw his way inside.

Taking a light pack Arnie climbed from the gorge and began his long journey. The snow-capped peaks turned golden in the early morning sun. He moved steadily, his body in much better shape than when he had come in. But even so the trail was hard to follow. Every rock pile looked the same.

He remembered the meadow when he came upon it. He remembered the tale of the bears his uncle had told; fresh bear droppings and broken bushes were an uncomfortable reminder. He even fancied he could smell the rancid odour of their bodies. Arnie needed rest, but he didn't want to stay there.

Instead, he cut down the mountain and, scrambling on top of a granite shoulder, looked towards the sea of peaks in the general direction of home — and help. There were so many! They were so far! He got tired all over again thinking about it.

If he could only find a trail that led to something. His shoulders sagged.

From the tip of a burned tree trunk a brown bird sang but Arnie didn't hear it. He was worrying about his uncle. His imagination was so vivid that he could almost hear the rip of cedar shakes torn apart by wolverine claws.

As he got his breath back he began to remember something. A road in the bottom of the valley. But was it the deep valley below him, or some other wide valley behind yet another mountain further on? His head began to ache, but he made a decision. He would head down.

He climbed over fallen tree trunks while black flies bit him and danced before his eyes. The ground was so rough and the going so hard that his legs felt like jelly.

The wind began to blow. Thunderheads gathered and broke. Huddling in the shelter of an overhanging rock, he was overtaken by sleep. When he awoke the sky was clear and full of stars and the air bit with chill.

Arnie shook himself, confused. Carefully he crept from his shelter and stood up straight. The stars above him were so plain he could almost touch them. The far peaks were sharp and gleaming. But one star was out of place. It moved, far down below him . . .

Now he knew what it was. The headlights of a car. A car . . . A road! Help!

Arnie shouted and began to run. But you can't run down a mountain. He picked himself up and impatiently waited for morning, moving his arms and stamping his feet while the cold air bit in.

He was lucky. He broke from the bush at the roadside just as a park warden drove by. The truck stopped. Arnie had found his help.

There's a small mine now near Crazy Creek, just out of park boundaries. Arnie owns it, with his Uncle Bill. *The Wolverine.* That's a good name for a mine.

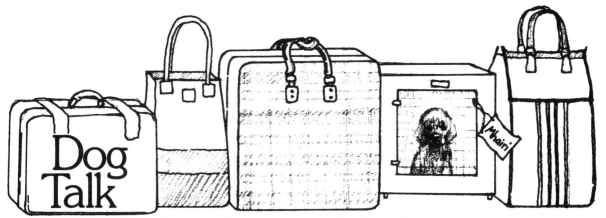

Dog Talk

by: Audrey Stewart   illustration: Nancy Lou Reynolds

Every dog I have owned has enjoyed the art of conversation. Each has responded with gratitude to a few softly spoken words which, when combined with a gentle touch on the head, particularly in the region of the ear, play a vital part in the building of a unique relationship.

Dogs vary greatly in the responses they show. A slight turn of the head and a brightening of the eyes usually means you have captured your dog's attention. A sigh, a yawn, a slight flaring of the nostrils, an almost imperceptible movement of the tongue, a notable increase in the rate of respiration, a batting of the paw — all these have their own special significance which you will learn to recognize.

My dog is a jet-black, one hundred and seventy pound, purebred Newfoundland. She prefers to be spoken to from one side or the other rather than face to face. She likes to feel free either to meet my direct gaze by turning her head or to take on an air of detachment, appearing only slightly interested. She is always a ready listener, her enjoyment being enhanced by frequent pauses in my flow of words, thus allowing her time to signify her understanding in her own special way.

Mhairi (pronounced VAREE, her name being of Gaelic origin), has one favourite ritual. Like a child, she never tires of tales of her own babyhood, recounted again and again, with the same rise and fall of the voice, the same choice of words and the same number of pauses. She has learned to sit with a particular "tell me a story about when I was a baby" look on her face. It is unmistakable and we both understand the significance of it.

"Mhairi," I say softly, moving closer to her side and with my cheek almost touching her face, "do you remember the night you arrived in Ontario from your native island of Newfoundland?" A flicker of the ears and slight turn of the head and I know she is with me. "It was a cold day in January when you left that snowy outport of Harbour Grace in your cosy little travel-box." I pause. I am always careful to avoid any mention of her warm, furry mother or her fluffy brothers and sisters and I make no reference to the obvious ordeal of a puppy's first jet flight. Even so, at this point I always notice a slight drawing in of the tongue and a momentary expression of strain passes over Mhairi's face. "And, Mhairi," I continue, "do you remember how that little travel-box got mixed up with all the suitcases in Terminal Two at Toronto and was placed by mistake on the baggage carousel?" Another pause. She snuggles closer to me in happy anticipation of the next few words. "I was worried sick, Mhairi. I was there waiting for you and you were there waiting for me but neither of us could find each other. Oh Mhairi, I was worried sick." I pause and am rewarded with a batting of the paw and a lick on my hand and her face relaxes again. "I had begun to think that you were not going to arrive at all. I had begun to think that somehow that little travel-box with that little black puppy inside had got lost and I would never see it." Another lick. "But suddenly, quite by chance, I turned into the building where the baggage carousel was going round and round and round and round. And there, on that carousel, Oh Mhairi, what joy, what relief! There you were. How long had you been there? Neither of us knows. Round and round and round and round." A pause. Her breathing becomes a little more rapid for a moment but she soon settles again and, with a gentle push of her nose, prods me to continue.

"Out of the box you came, Mhairi, and into my arms. How I loved you! How I love you! We had found each other. This is the end of the story, Mhairi, but for you and for me it was just the beginning."

I pause for several seconds. Then she stands up, licks my face, sighs and walks away happy. Very happy.

Susan Super Sleuth:

Christmas Chase

by: William Ettridge   *illustrations: Laura Piotrowski*

"There's a vacant spot — over there." Susan pointed across the crowded underground car park. "Where those two men are standing next to the blue van," she added.

"I see it." Her mother drove to the end of the aisle, swung round the double row of cars, and headed back toward the blue van. "Oh no, you don't!" she muttered as she slipped into the vacant space, forestalling the intentions of another driver who raced his car toward them, ignoring the directional arrows painted on the floor. The other vehicle narrowly missed them, the driver's face distorted as he snarled in their direction.

"Well done, Mother." Susan released her seat belt.

"Perhaps I should have let him have the spot," her mother mused. "After all, it is Christmas time, the season of goodwill."

"Perhaps it is — " Susan turned and reached in the rear seat for her purse " — but we've spent the last ten minutes driving around following the arrows as we should. Why should he just drive in, ignore the rules, and be rewarded by finding a spot immediately?"

The other driver had stopped and reversed his car, and now sat parked behind them in the aisle. The two men had moved from their position beside the blue van, and were now stooped, talking to the driver through his open window.

"They're sinister looking characters, aren't they?"

"Hush, dear." Her mother opened her door. "We've a lot of shopping to do, so hurry along."

"I do believe that driver's wearing a wig," Susan muttered as she too stepped from the car. "Red eyebrows and black hair just don't match." She closed her door, glanced once more at the trio, who were checking their watches, then hurried to follow her mother to the elevator.

"I just love this time of the year." Susan's eyes shone with pleasure as she raised her voice above the din of moving traffic, shuffling

feet, piped music, and the babble of a hundred conversations, as they moved slowly through the crowds of Christmas shoppers. "Shall we stop for a coffee?"

"Good idea." Her mother glanced at her watch. "I've only got to buy batteries for this flashlight." She waved their last purchase. "Then we'll be finished."

"Right." Susan drew her mother to a halt. "You grab a table," she said, pointing into a restaurant, "and I'll dash into the hardware store next door for the batteries. Two 'D' size, isn't it?"

"That's a relief." Susan dropped into a chair. "My feet are complaining." Pulling out a vacant seat she marshalled their packages into a compact pile. Sitting back, she glanced around at

the other tables. "You were fortunate to get this table so quickly — the restaurant's packed."

There was a bustle of movement three tables away as a couple stood up, gathered their belongings, and headed for the door. Idly, Susan watched their progress, but then her attention was drawn to a man who moved to occupy the vacant table, a cup of coffee in his hand.

She leaned toward her mother. "That horrible man from the car park has just come in."

"Is that right, dear?" Her mother concentrated on sugaring her coffee.

"Yes. And the more I look at him, the less I like. He's definitely wearing a wig; his own hair is peeking out just behind the ears." She peered at the man's neck and ears. "That's something I've not seen before."

"What's that?" Susan's mother gingerly removed the cover from a cream container.

"One ear has a distinctive lobe, but the other hasn't; it just blends directly into his head." She quickly dropped her eyes as the man turned his head, but not before she noticed how piercing his grey eyes appeared under frowning red brows. "I wonder where he's off to now?" Susan watched the man stand up and thread his way between the tables.

"Where do you think?" her mother answered as she glanced over her shoulder.

"Silly me!" Susan chuckled as the man slipped through a plainly marked door.

"If you've finished your coffee, Sue, we should start for home." She dabbed at her mouth with her napkin. "I'll just go and freshen up — I'll not be a minute. Now, don't leave anything behind. There's a parcel there, here's another, and your coat . . ."

"It's quite all right, Mother. I'll collect everything." She smiled fondly at her mother's departing back. Dear old Mum; she seemed to forget that her daughter was no longer an irresponsible six-year-old. After collecting their belongings Susan moved to wait close to the restroom doors.

She waited patiently for several minutes. Then, just as she turned to enter the ladies' restroom and hurry her mother, the adjacent door swung open and the man brushed past, hands occupied in fitting a pair of glasses. Susan spun on her heel to follow his progress through the restaurant. A frown wrinkled her brow. What was different? Of course! He'd changed his coat. Before it had been brown; now it was dark blue — obviously a reversible garment. But why? Why change his appearance by donning thick-rimmed glasses, wearing a wig, and switching his coat? Unless . . .

"Ah! There you are. Quickly!" Susan grasped the arm of her bewildered mother and dragged her in pursuit of the man.

"What, we . . ." her mother stammered. "Sorry. Excuse me . . ." She spattered apologies as, pulled along by Susan, she accidently bumped into unwary shoppers.

"Where is he? Where is he?" Susan stepped through the door onto the crowded sidewalk. "Oh, heck!" There was no sign of her quarry; he'd disappeared into the bustling crowd.

"Young lady." Her mother straightened her hat. "Would you mind telling me what that was all about?"

"That man! The man in the car park," she added in explanation. "There's something fishy about him. He's wearing a wig, heavy glasses, and he's changed his coat — he's in disguise!" Her voice rose excitedly. "He's up to something — I just know he is."

"Really, Susan! It's getting late, and there really isn't time for you to take us on a wild goose chase."

"We've lost him anyway." Susan took a last regretful look along the sidewalk. "Come along then, Mother. I want to make just one more purchase, at the bakery, and then we'll head for home."

Fifteen minutes later, their shopping completed, they stepped out of the bakery and turned toward the car park. It was quite dark now, but under the bright street lights the shopping crowds were as great as ever as they moved past the decorated store windows.

Suddenly the strident peal of a burglar alarm filled the air. For a moment there was a pause in the moving crowd, but, as is usually the case, the majority assumed it was a false alarm and continued on their way.

Unable to hurry in the press, Susan nevertheless urged her mother toward the persistent ringing — it might well be a genuine alarm! Looking ahead over the top of the crowds she could see the sign of a goldsmith high on the wall of a building at the next intersection. Then, distant at first, but rapidly drawing near, they heard the rising and falling siren of a police cruiser. Traffic pulled to the nearside lane as, with flashing lights, not one, but two police cars raced by, brake lights flaring as they screeched to a stop. Moving faster now as the crowd thronged toward the scene, Susan and her mother soon found themselves at the road junction, further progress barred by the densely packed onlookers. Frustrated in their efforts to move closer, they edged sideways along a side street, flanked by offices and warehouses, to where the crowd had thinned. Automatically scanning the throng for a person or persons not acting in a normal manner, Susan caught a movement in the corner of her eye. She turned her head and peered down the darker side street. Yes! There, about fifty yards away, but on the opposite side of the road, a dark vehicle was slowly moving away. Raising her hand to shield her eyes from the street lights overhead, she could make out two figures pushing a small van. A muffled report sounded as an engine started and the van jerked forward. One of the men ran and climbed into it, but the other stumbled and fell as it moved away from him. Just as he jumped to his feet, another vehicle swung into the poorly lit sidestreet, its headlights briefly illuminating the scene.

"Look, Mother. It's him!" Quite clearly they saw the man in the dark blue coat, glasses flashing in the sweeping beams as he glanced back over his shoulder.

Apparently panicked by the approaching car, the driver of the van sped off before Blue-coat could climb aboard, leaving him

to chase hopelessly after it.

"Come on, Susan!" This time her mother took the initiative. "We'll follow him. If those men set off the alarm, it's our duty to see where they go. Obviously no one else saw the van leaving," she added in justification.

"Good for you, Mother." Susan was delighted that her mother now shared her suspicions. Grasping their packages mother and daughter moved quickly to follow the man.

In a short while he crossed to their side of the street, and a few yards further along slipped into a narrow passage.

"Heading to the car park I think," Susan's mother panted, slightly out of breath, but quite exhilarated by the chase.

They turned into the passage to find themselves much closer to their quarry; he was now walking. Suddenly however, perhaps because he had heard the clicking of their heels, he glanced back. Seeing their figures clearly outlined against the passage opening, he broke into a trot. Hampered as they were with their packages, Susan and her mother fell behind. The man reached the end of the passage, emerging onto a major thoroughfare; he turned right, out of their sight.

"Quickly." Susan too was panting.

They reached the main road in their turn, just in time to see the man cross over and disappear, not into the car park, but into the shell of a new office block under construction next door.

Delayed for a few moments by a stream of traffic, mother and daughter also crossed the road, and hurried to the building.

"In here. This is where he went." Susan made to step behind a sheet of wood pulled aside from where it had covered a doorless opening. "You find a policeman, Mother," she instructed.

"Oh, no!" Her mother was not going to be left behind. "I'm coming with you."

Packages hindering their efforts, they squeezed through the narrow opening, then stood quietly, ears straining for the slightest sound. Gradually their eyes became accustomed to the half-light of street lamps shining in through window openings high above their heads. They found themselves in a large, bare, concrete entrance hall. A flight of stairs climbed to their right, blocked after several treads by a sheet of corrugated steel.

"He didn't go up, so he must be in there." Susan pointed to an archway on their left.

Her mother fumbled with her parcels.

"Where did I . . . Ah, here it is." A click, and a flashlight beam stabbed across the room.

"I'm very glad you bought that," Susan observed.

"So am I," her mother answered feelingly.

Shoulders touching for mutual courage, they stepped across to the arched opening. The flashlight played along a broad passage leading into the core of the building. Susan moved ahead, eager to sight their quarry.

"Susan!" her mother hissed. "Slow down. We don't want to catch up with him; he might be dangerous!"

"I think we've lost him." Susan halted as the passage curved to the right before ending, a smaller corridor striking off at right angles in each direction. "Which way did he go?" She dithered, moving first one way and then the other.

"Ssh!" her mother urged. "Listen!"

They stood as if made of stone, ears cocked for the slightest sound. Nothing. Nothing but the distant murmur of an occasional vehicle passing the front of the building.

Then. "Did you hear that?" Her mother grasped Susan's elbow. "There it is again." She moved to the left, Susan close behind.

Faintly a grating sound was repeated. The sound of brick or stone sliding across the cement floor. Then quite clearly there was the thud of a closing door. Sure now of their direction they moved along together, thoughts of possible danger quite forgotten in the excitement of the chase.

"Careful, Mum," Susan warned as they came upon a mass of broken bricks strewn across the floor.

They picked their way past the obstacle, passing a number of doorless rooms, each of which they swept with the flashlight before passing on.

"Oops!" Just in time Susan stopped as the floor fell away to a flight of steps leading downwards. Momentarily they hesitated. Raising the flashlight to illuminate both faces, Susan's mother raised her eyebrows in question. Her daughter shrugged her shoulders and raised her eyebrows in turn. Unspoken, the dilemma flashed between them. Go on, or retrace their steps? Together they nodded their heads. On it would be!

Susan took the flashlight, and for a split second they were plunged into total blackness as it changed hands. That momentary taste of darkness sent a sobering tingle up their spines, reminding them of the very real danger of chasing a possible criminal through the echoing tomb of the unfinished building.

Slower now, they crept down the steps. " . . . nine, ten . . . " Susan counted under her breath. " . . . seventeen . . ." And lastly " . . . eighteen." They were now some four metres below ground level. The lower corridor was short; less than ten paces from the foot of the steps to where they were stopped by a plain closed door.

Gently, Susan grasped a lever-like handle with the hand holding the flashlight, the other grasping her parcels. The light beam swept up the wall at her side as the handle moved under her touch. Slowly she pushed the door open; it was heavy and very thick, a steel-faced fire door. What if the man was waiting for them? She glanced back at her mother's shadowy figure, and a smile curved her lips. Her mother was ready, a half brick raised threateningly in her hand, poised to strike if danger leapt out at them.

Decisively, Susan stepped smartly backward, thrusting the door open as she did. With a bang it swung through a hundred and eighty degrees to crash against the wall. They waited, muscles tensed. Nothing. Nothing but the sound of her mother's breathing. Surprised, Susan realized that she herself was holding her breath — she let it out in a long sigh. With some reluctance they edged forward, the flashlight beam swinging from side to side as they entered what appeared to be a store room. Lengths of pipe lay scattered on the floor together with reels of electrical cable, piles of sacking, and several packing cases. They hesitated. The man *had* to be behind one of the cases; there were no other doors. Susan swung the light towards the ceiling. There *was* no ceiling! It wasn't a store room after all. They were standing at the foot of an elevator shaft, which tapered away to blackness above their heads. Susan could see door openings piercing one wall at regular intervals, the lowest well out of reach. Dropping the beam she played it over the largest packing case, about two metres square by a metre high.

Crash! They whirled around as the door slammed shut! Together they threw themselves at the steel-faced barrier. There was no handle; just the central stem on which the handle had been pinned. There was no way they could turn it.

"Hey! Let us out!" Susan pounded on the door.

"Having trapped us in here, he's not about to let us out again," her mother observed. She moved to the large crate and divested herself of her packages.

Susan turned the light on her mother. "I must say, you're taking it all very calmly."

"There's no point in getting upset, is there, dear?"

Good old Mum, always calm in a crisis!

"How did he get behind us?" Susan mused. She too moved to the packing case and piled her shopping with her mother's. "Of course!" she snorted in self disgust. "Now I remember. The stairs were narrower than the corridor, and there was a space to one side. That's where we missed him. He must have hidden under the stairs. Ugh! How stupid of me."

There was a rustle of paper. She turned to see her mother perched on top of the case.

"What are you doing? Hey! Those cakes were for tomorrow. How can you just sit there eating?"

"Um. They're rather nice. Well, my dear —" her mother licked her fingers "— when I get concerned I get hungry, and if I don't nibble something I'll probably scream, because I'm just a little bit scared. How do you think we'll get out of here? We could be stuck for days!"

"I don't know," Susan admitted. "But between us, I'm sure we'll come up with a way." She switched off the light, and in a few minutes their eyes became adjusted to the faint luminosity filtering down from the lowermost opening in the shaft. Hoisting herself up beside her mother, Susan helped herself to cake. "If I don't grab one now, I can see that you'll eat them all," she observed as her mother rustled the bag once again.

They sat in companionable silence, busy with their own thoughts for a short while. Finally Susan crumpled the empty bag.

"You know, we've got to get out of here within the next hour or so. I'm quite sure that man was involved with that alarm . . ."

"He wouldn't run off if he wasn't guilty of something," her mother interrupted, "and he certainly wouldn't have locked us in here."

"I think he burgled the goldsmith's, slipped out of the side door, rendezvoused with the men in the blue van, and planned to make a clean getaway."

"I think you may be right. Unless we get to the police before they cross the border, that's just what they will do."

"So you noticed the New York licence plate on the van?"

"You didn't inherit your detective skills just from your father, you know!" her mother reminded her. "I *did* earn my Girl Guide badges for

tracking and observation," she added with a chuckle.

"Okay, marvellous Mum, how do we get out?" Susan's chuckle joined her mother's.

"Not through the door obviously, so it has to be up there." She pointed to the lowest opening.

"Agreed." Susan jumped down. Switching on the flashlight she swept the beam around their prison and took stock of the material littering the floor. "Perhaps we could make a rope of electrical cable, tie it to a piece of pipe, then throw the pipe up to jam across the opening."

"That's an awful long way to throw a piece of steel pipe," her mother observed. "Now if we could climb on top of that pipe sticking out of the wall. No, higher up," she directed as Susan pointed the beam at the wall. "Just about eye level."

Susan stepped across to the large pipe jutting from the wall, a large wheel protruding from one side.

"It's a water main or something." Susan reached up and grasped the wheel. After some initial resistance it moved under her hand. A few drops of water fell from the gaping mouth. She turned the wheel further, and the drops became a trickle, then a flood. She spun the valve closed.

"We'd still be too low even if we could stand on it, and I'm sure I couldn't keep my balance and throw a pipe up to the opening." She nibbled at her thumb as she fell into deep thought.

"Could we pile these crates high enough?" her mother suggested.

"No, I don't thi . . . Just a minute!" She stepped swiftly to her mother's side. "They're wooden, and — " she kicked the side, producing a hollow sound " — yes, empty. It'll probably work."

"Susan, as your mother I've learned to anticipate many of your antics, but I'm not a mind reader. *What* will probably work?"

"This. I'll turn on the water full force. We'll sit on top of the crate, and after a while we'll just float up until we reach that opening." She picked up a piece of sacking and stuffed it along the bottom of the door. "I'll seal this off as best I can. We'll be up and out in no time."

"But how much time?" Her mother dropped from the box and, picking up a length of pipe, attacked one of the smaller crates. "Paddles," she explained in answer to Susan's questioning cough.

"Good idea," Susan agreed. "Well now, time. A big main pipe like this should deliver at least a thousand litres a minute, which is the same as a cubic metre. This room measures about four metres in each direction, and we need to float up three metres or so. So, we'll need four times four, times three . . . er, that's forty-eight cubic metres of water, and that would be forty-eight minutes." She turned the big wheel, spinning it until the water was gushing in a great arching curve. Quickly she scrambled to join her mother on top of the crate, feet drawn clear of the ground.

"I just can't work in metric," said Susan's mother. She gathered the parcels well clear of the edges of the crate. "But using the old system, if this room is thirteen feet square, and we need to go up ten feet, we'll need . . . um — " she multiplied mentally "— about seventeen hundred cubic feet of water, and that's about eleven thousand gallons. If the water is coming in at a thousand litres a minute, what's that in gallons?"

"Approximately two hundred and twenty I think."

"Then we need to divide eleven thousand by two hundred and twenty. That's fifty, isn't it? Yes it is," she answered herself decisively. "Fifty minutes — your fifty-one sounds close enough."

"I can see why we switched to metric!" Susan shouted. "We could drown in the time it takes to work out a sum like that." The cascading water was deafening now.

Shortly, just as Susan moved a leg to relieve a cramp, they felt the crate stir under them. The water had risen two-thirds up the sides of the container, and now they were afloat. Hopefully they would eventually be able to clamber out of the shaft without getting their feet wet.

Gradually the water rose until the outlet pipe was below the surface, and the roar of the water fell away to nothing. It was much easier to talk now. They chatted idly, the time dragging as they waited to float high enough to reach the opening. Susan occupied herself with plaiting a wire rope which she attached to a piece of pipe, and which she planned to jam across the opening.

It became apparent that Susan had overestimated the rate of water flow. Nearly an hour after she had turned on the water they were still far from being able to merely step out at ground level. Another fifteen minutes passed. Susan moved impatiently.

"This is no good, Mother. I'm going to see if I can reach by standing up."

"Careful!" her mother warned, as the wooden case dipped alarmingly. "Let's paddle closer to the wall; then you'll be able to steady yourself."

Together they gingerly paddled their

unstable craft until it touched the wall below the opening. Slowly Susan climbed to her knees, the case rocking under her movement. Then, with her mother paddling to maintain their position, she eased herself to her feet. She reached up. Yes! Just. Her fingers curled over the door sill. She reached back with one hand, and her mother passed up the pipe and wire rope. She raised it above her head, and, almost spilling herself into the water with her efforts, managed to slide it out through the doorway until it firmly jammed into position. A few strokes of the paddle to push the case close against the wall once more, a tug to ensure that the pipe was secure, and Susan quickly scaled her way out of the shaft. She turned to help her mother.

"What on earth are you doing?" She had expected to see her mother close behind, but instead she was offering up packages.

"If you think I'm going to leave this shopping here after carrying it this far . . ."

Susan shook her head in exasperation. "Really, Mum!" But she relieved her mother of the packages. A few seconds later, her mother at her side, Susan pushed open an emergency door and they spilled out on to the main road.

"Hey there! Hey!" Susan jumped into the road, one arm full of packages, the other waving wildly at a police cruiser passing by on the opposite side. "Help!" she shouted at the top of her voice. The white blur of the driver's face turned in her direction. There was a screech of brakes as the car came to a smoky halt. Neatly the cruiser wheeled in a U-turn to slide to a stop at her side.

The next morning brought seasonable weather. Cutting sleet carried on a blustery northern wind. Susan settled down with a crossword puzzle after helping her mother with the breakfast dishes, chased out of the kitchen for stealing hot mince pies. Uncle Ted, her police inspector uncle, was expected for lunch, and she hoped that he would bring good news. Acting on the description of the van, police had arrested two men just before they crossed the border into the United States at Niagara Falls, but Blue-coat had not been spotted. Under a false floor in the rear of the van the police had found a large quantity of gold rings, charms and other jewellery, easily identified as being taken from the Yonge Street goldsmith.

Susan's detailed description of the third man, especially of the peculiar unmatched ear lobes, had resulted in the police naming a

suspect, but he had yet to be apprehended. He was known to police forces of both Canada and the United States, so hopefully he had been picked up by now.

The time passed slowly as Susan worked her way through the puzzle. One clue she simply could not solve. About to throw the paper down in disgust, she heard the ring of the door bell.

"I'll get it," she called as she rushed to the door.

She could tell immediately that Uncle Ted had good news; his eyes were twinkling. He refused to say a word, however, until he had greeted Susan's mother and father, and insisted that she make him a hot drink. As he said, it was the least he deserved for fighting his way through the terrible weather.

Finally, sitting himself in the chair formerly occupied by Susan, coffee cup in hand, he relented.

"Yes, we picked him up this morning trying to cross the border at Fort Erie. You'll have to attend a police line-up, but I'm sure he's the right man."

"Isn't that good, Mum?" Susan appealed to her mother, who stood just inside the door wiping her floury hands on her apron. "All wrapped up for Christmas."

Idly, Uncle Ted picked up the crossword puzzle. "Now what's this? One clue unanswered! Don't tell me that our super-sleuth is stuck?"

"Yuck!" Susan answered with feeling.

" 'Vat floats here in car housing,' " Uncle Ted read out. "Looks like an anagram to me." He took a pencil from his pocket. "Yes, we need two words, one with eight letters, and one with five. 'Van floats here' has thirteen letters, and we'll have to rearrange them for the answer."

He puzzled away for a while before sending Susan to refill his cup. As she was returning she was startled to hear loud peals of laughter from her parents and Uncle Ted.

"What's so funny?" she demanded as she entered the room.

"This, the last answer to your crossword," Uncle Ted explained. "Shame on you, Susan! You should have solved it; you've had enough experience." Once more the adults' laughter rang out.

Susan hurried to look over her uncle's shoulder.

"Oh no!" She threw up her hands. " 'Elevator shaft!' "

The Elusive Secret of Oak Island

by: Jean Booker   *illustrations: Don Inman*

The underwater camera is lowered down a 230-foot shaft. Nearby a man watches on a closed-circuit monitor. Suddenly, what seems to be a human hand appears on the screen. The scene changes and three wooden chests come into view, followed by a picture of a human body propped against a wall of the underground cavern.

Sounds like a hair-raising adventure tale? It is. It's part of the story of a search for hidden treasure on Oak Island, a search that has been going on for almost two hundred years.

Oak Island is about forty miles southwest of Halifax and is one of a group of over three hundred islands in Mahone Bay on the Atlantic coast of Nova Scotia. The island is one mile long and half a mile across at its widest point.

In the summer of 1795 a teenage boy was exploring uninhabited Oak Island when he noticed something unusual. In the middle of a clearing there was a huge oak tree with a branch about fifteen feet up that was cut off four feet from the trunk. Beneath this branch was a depression twelve feet in diameter. The next day the boy went back to the island with two friends. Using picks and shovels, they dug below the tree and discovered the soil was loose. At a depth of two feet the young men found a layer of flagstones, and, on removing them, realized they were digging in a round shaft more than seven feet wide. It looked as if the sawn off oak branch above could have been used originally to help remove the earth from this shaft.

The young men continued digging for several days and were surprised to find snugly fitting platforms of oak logs across the pit every ten feet to a depth of thirty feet. They felt sure that pirate treasure was buried there, but when it wasn't discovered at the thirty foot level, they gave up their search. However, two of them bought land lots on Oak Island and all three kept looking for many more years.

Seven years later — in 1802 — another try was made to find the treasure, this time by a Truro company. Machinery was brought to Oak Island and the original pit was re-excavated to a depth of ninety feet. Oak platforms were again found every ten feet and quantities of charcoal, putty and coconut fibre. The presence of coconut fibre was interesting because, while Oak Island is about fifteen hundred miles away from the closest coconut tree, ships in the sixteenth century used the fibre as packing round cargo to prevent water damage.

Ninety feet down the workers found a big flat stone with strange carvings on the bottom. These carvings were later deciphered to read, "Ten feet below are two million pounds buried." But where is this stone now? Unfortunately it has disappeared.

That evening, after removing the stone, the workers were sure they were about to find the treasure. But on returning early the following morning, they found instead sixty feet of water in the shaft! Efforts to bail out the water failed, and the men eventually gave up as some of them had farms to look after and couldn't neglect them any longer.

The next year the company returned and this time dug a new shaft fourteen feet southeast of the original one. From this shaft they hoped to tunnel through to the first one and reach the treasure. They got to a depth of one hundred and ten feet and were within two feet of the first shaft when the water flooded in. Two hours later the water in the new shaft measured sixty-five feet. The water was salty and seemed to rise and fall with the ocean tides. Somehow the sea was getting into the shafts, but how?

Water continued to foil other explorations over the years. It was discovered that Smith's Cove Beach, which was about five hundred feet east of the original shaft, was not a natural beach, but was composed of tons of coconut fibre several inches deep, underneath the sand between the low and high tide lines. Beneath the coconut fibre was eel grass and a layer of beach rocks packed tightly together. Efforts to build a stone and clay cofferdam to hold back the tides failed, but led to the discovery of five fan-shaped drains under the beach. These drains were eventually thought to be part of a huge feeder system which allowed sea water to enter the original shaft at a rate of six hundred gallons per minute.

Who constructed these underground tunnels and why? The answers to these questions have still to be found. Most theories centre around buried pirate treasure. It is estimated that the original work on Oak Island must have taken about 100,000 man-hours! It was obviously an important project, yet to date no one has come up with any concrete answers or any real signs of buried treasure. Could the treasure have been removed years ago, or is it still there? Or was there ever any treasure at all?

A company called Triton Alliance Ltd. is trying to solve the Oak Island mystery. They were the ones who lowered the underwater camera into Borehole 10-X in August, 1971, and took photographs of the mysterious human hand. Unfortunately these photographs are not clear, but a Montreal physiologist felt that one of the pictures taken off the monitor could have been that of a human body, and a Halifax pathologist stated that human flesh could be preserved in a damp airless place.

Further exploration of Borehole 10-X by professional divers revealed a large cave at the bottom of the hole, but visibility was very bad. It was too dangerous for the divers to explore it fully, and in November, 1976, the shaft caved in.

So far, since 1795, approximately $2,000,000 have been spent trying to discover the elusive secret of Oak Island — but the mystery remains.

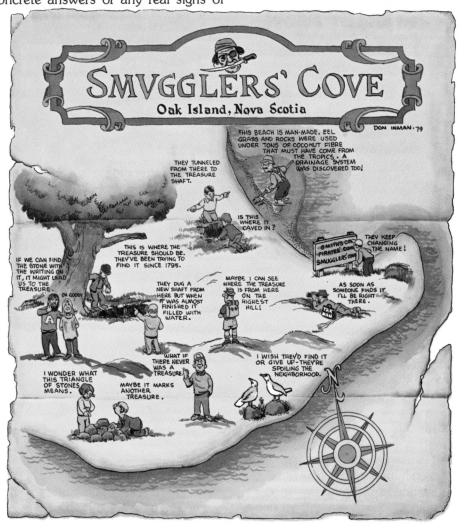

Autumn-Mobile

by: Alan Bradley   illustrations: Paul McCusker   (Title illustration: J.O. Radford)

Once, about twenty-thousand Thursdays ago (which isn't very long in time — but is very long indeed as Thursdays go), there was a land called Dulcina.

Now, the people of that place had chosen this name above all others because in their language, "Dulcina" meant *Green Home.* And a green home it was: green hill folded away after green hill into the green distance, where green shadows of green clouds moved slowly along beneath a green sky, where a green sun shone brightly (but greenly), its light sparkling like emeralds where it struck green reflections from the green ripples of a green sea. And when the sun was gone, a green moon (which was said by some to be made of green cheese) spread its soft green light into the soft, green night. Then the great green owls would stretch their wings, blink round, green eyes, and lean forward into the breeze of evening, to swoop silently over the dark landscape, hoping to catch a small green hedge-mouse as it took a bed-time walk.

In the day, when owls were abed, the green-cobbled streets of town and village were filled with noisy shrieks of children at their play, and the happy cries of workmen. A carpenter called down to his green-aproned apprentice to lug up yet another great green keg of green nails. They would have to hurry, he said, to have this greenhouse finished before nightfall — before the green rain.

And in the shipping-ports, the jolly sailors sang while they knotted fat green ropes to secure the green sailing-ships; then they filled green nets with green bananas, which would soon be hanging in the windows of every greengrocer's in the land. The sailors' songs were ancient ones:

Greensleeves was one; *Green Grow the Rushes — O* was another.

High above a village green, a sculptor in stone hummed to himself the tune of *Robin Greenwood* as he gouged another gargoyle from the green stone of the cathedral.

Anyway — you get the idea — the people were happy and almost everything was green.

And so it went, until one day — and a Thursday at that — a stranger arrived in the land of Dulcina.

The stranger's name was Fflatt — with two "f's" — and his arrival caused a sensation, to say the very least, for the carriage in which he was riding was not drawn by horses, but appeared to be propelled by some strange and invisible force — a force whose presence was indicated by a soft *Ploop-Ploop*-ing sound which came from a rusty bit of metal tubing that hung out from the rear of his strange vehicle. Also there was an occasional puff of venomous-smelling steam.

"My Ffriends . . ." cried Fflatt, standing up on the seat of his amazing machine. "My Ffriends . . ." (And when he spoke, his voice had a sharp and nasty sound, like air hissing from a pneumatic tire. No one recognized the sound, of course, for in that time pneumatic tires were still many thousands of Thursdays in the future.) "My Ffriends, I bring you good news — *great* news! And what *is* it, you ask?"

No one had asked anything, but Fflatt, in the way of all strangers in stories, was not easily put off by silence.

"There is a land . . ." he shouted, as the villagers gathered. "There is a land where the

"Aahhhh!" breathed the crowd — for crowds, just as they are too easily angered, are sometimes too easily satisfied.

"Now listen, my Ffriends," went on Fflatt, "these blue skies can easily be yours — for a consideration, of course. For a few trifling groats, you too can have skies of blue."

In a moment the crowd had picked up the phrase, and were repeating it with delight to one another, even as Fflatt reached down into the back seat of his curious machine and pulled out a large sign, whose garish letters read: YOU TOO CAN HAVE SKIES OF BLUE.

Within hours, word of this phenomenon had spread across the land of Dulcina, and in every town and village the Elders gathered by the light of green candles to talk it over.

In the morning, as green daybreak appeared, messengers arrived from every corner of the land, each bringing the same question: "How many groats for skies of blue?"

"Only a few," said Fflatt. "Six million, five-hundred thousand, nine hundred and eighty-six. *Gold* groats, that is."

Now the messengers reversed their paths and sped away with Fflatt's offer.

In the green evening, courting couples strolled round and round the village green, reading at each passage Fflatt's sign, which now hung nailed between two ancient elms. YOU TOO CAN HAVE SKIES OF BLUE, it said.

Then the messengers were back.

"Yes!" they shouted. "Yes! Yes! Yes!" and each of them delivered to Fflatt a heavy bag of gold.

"Give us our blue skies," they demanded.

"Not yet," said Fflatt. "First I count my gold — *then* you get your blue."

For twenty-seven days they waited while Fflatt carefully counted — then *re*-counted — and *re-re*-counted the coins. Only then was he satisfied.

"Tomorrow morning," he announced, "I will give you your blue skies."

As the green sun arose from behind the green hills, a silent crowd gathered to watch Fflatt, who, after making a brief speech on the wonders and benefits of blue, strode to his machine and whisked away a covering of tarpaulin that had hidden its sides.

There, for all to see, in foot-high letters, was painted: THE GENUINE ORIGINAL AUTUMN-MOBILE.

Without a word, Fflatt began to unroll a long series of flexible tubes and hoses,

skies are *blue*! Strange, but true. I've seen it with my own eyes!"

"Blue?" muttered Old Greenleaf, the village schoolmaster. "What do you mean? What is blue?"

"The *sky*, my learned Ffriend," shouted Fflatt. "The *sky* is blue."

"But what *is* blue?" persisted Old Greenleaf.

"A colour, my Ffriend — blue is a colour."

"What kind of colour?"

"A kind of . . . *blue* colour, my Ffriend — a *new* colour. Can't you imagine a new colour, one you've never seen before?"

Old Greenleaf had to admit he couldn't, nor could anyone else in the village.

"Describe it to us, then," cried Greenough, the baker.

"Oh! Simple, simple task," smiled Fflatt. "Blue is a colour — a *new* colour!"

"He can't do it," snickered Greenaway, who shod the great green horses, and called himself a greensmith.

"Silence!" shouted Fflatt. "Give the stranger his due. Blue is *easily* described: blue is that hue which is *not* green."

and connected them, with the aid of a small hand-drill, to the roots of each and every tree in the village.

Within a few hours he was out of sight; over the green hills, spooling his endless tubes behind him.

In the evening, as the green sun dipped below the horizon, Fflatt was back. He began a complicated series of adjustments to the valves that linked his vast network of tubes to the Autumn-Mobile. From time to time he called out orders to himself, as if he were directing the labours of a mighty army.

"EASY, NOW — EASY!" he shouted, turning a tap.

"STEADY — REPORT FLOW!" he ordered.

"COMING UP — PRESSURE GOOD — FULL FLOW!" he replied; and all the while his strange machine thrummed and shook, hummed and quivered in the green twilight.

The villagers stood in smaller clusters now. A chill was in the air.

"Are you finished?" they asked.

"QUIET!" thundered Fflatt. "A bargain is as good as a deal. Go home to your beds, and in the morning — we'll see what we shall see."

Not wishing to anger this man — this Fflatt — who seemed to know what he was doing, they went; and lay in their beds awake, listening through the night to the incessant chuffing and the wheeze of the Autumn-Mobile.

Next morning, early as the sun, the cobbler's boy ran gasping through the streets. "Come and see!" he called. "He's done it! Come and see!"

One by one the villagers appeared, their eyes at first drooping with sleep — then wide with astonishment.

Above their heads, a sky of deepest blue spread from horizon to horizon. A yellow sun shone down among the radiant trees, each one a different shade of red, and orange, and of gold.

"Oh! Look at this colour!" they shouted. "No — look at that — and there — and here!"

Not until they had finished gasping in admiration did they see that the Autumn-Mobile had vanished. Of it and its owner there was not a trace.

"It's quite a lot of red," said the butcher after a while. "And that sky: so blue — that sun: so gold."

"And the air's too cool," complained the schoolmaster's wife. "I'm going in before I catch my death of cold."

Another found the leaves too dry, and another the colours too harsh. Soon, arguments broke out, and the Elders were assembled to hear the villagers' complaints. At length, having listened to this one and that one, rejecting here and sympathizing there, a common fault was found. It was this: there was no green.

A yellow sun shone down through white clouds in a blue sky. Brown grass surrounded every tree, whose rustling leaves were aflame with colour in the ever-cooling breeze.

The Elders said this:

"The sky is not the one we know. It is wrong. Each tree is a stranger to our eyes. Therefore, we will seek out this Fflatt, and make him restore our world. Though it cost us every groat we have, he will give us back our land. He will bring us back the green."

But of course, Fflatt was never seen again, and the land of Dulcina remained wrapped in perpetual autumn.

It is said that there's a corner of our minds containing scenes from long ago — from times that passed before we were born. Perhaps that's why, you and I, so many thousand Thursdays later, are not surprised each year, in fall, when we see the splendour of the leaves, to find in them a hint of ancient days, and of sadness. For then, we might remember Dulcina.

GRANT McCONACHIE'S FIRST JOB WAS WITH THE RAILROAD - HIS FATHER'S TRADE. AT FIRST HE WORKED ONLY IN THE SUMMERS BUT LATER BECAME A FULL-TIME EMPLOYEE. HE WORKED HIS WAY UP FROM ASH-WHEELER TO ENGINEER BUT SOON BECAME FASCINATED BY THE NORTH AND A NEW BREED OF ADVENTURERS - THE "BUSH PILOTS".

"..BEST NATURAL PILOT I'VE EVER SEEN!"

GRANT LEARNED TO FLY ON WEEKENDS. DURING THAT PART OF HIS LIFE TWO OF HIS STRONGEST CHARACTERISTICS BECAME EVIDENT - HIS GREAT NATURAL ABILITY TO FLY AN AIRPLANE AND AN UNUSUAL PENCHANT FOR GETTING INTO TROUBLE... AND THEN TALKING HIS WAY OUT OF IT.

GRANT'S UNCLE HARRY - THE FAMILY "BLACKSHEEP" - PUT UP $2,500.00 TO BUY A USED AIRCRAFT AND HE AND GRANT WERE IN THE FLYING BUSINESS! THEY WERE JOINED BY A MALTESE PRINCESS WHO ADDED TWO AIRCRAFT - AND A LOT OF COLOR - TO THE NEW COMPANY.

THEIR FIRST PAYLOAD WAS FOR A RESEARCH PROJECT ON MIGRATION. TWO HUNDRED CROWS WITH YELLOW-PAINTED TAILS WERE FLOWN SOUTH FROM EDMONTON AND RELEASED.
A NEW, LONGER-TERM CONTRACT SIGNALLED THE REAL START OF THEIR FREIGHT-HAULING BUSINESS. THEY UNDERTOOK TO FLY THIRTY THOUSAND POUNDS OF FISH A WEEK FROM LESSER SLAVE LAKE TO THE RAILHEAD AT BONNEYVILLE.

CRASH AT CALDER..!

ICE BUILD-UP ON THE PROPELLER CAUSED A NEAR-FATAL CRASH FOR GRANT IN NOVEMBER, 1932. AFTER TAKE-OFF THE PLANE LACKED POWER TO CLIMB. A SERIES OF HAIR-PIN TURNS AND NEAR MISSES OVER THE VILLAGE OF CALDER ENDED IN A CRASH IN AN OPEN FIELD. GRANT WAS SERIOUSLY INJURED AND SPENT TWO MONTHS IN HOSPITAL. HE NEARLY LOST HIS LEG. HE WAS HAILED AS A HERO IN THE NEWSPAPERS BECAUSE HE MANAGED TO AVOID THE HOMES AND BUILDINGS OF THE TOWN.

TO BUY A "FORD TRI-MOTOR" OWNED BY MINING MILLIONAIRE SIR HARRY OAKES, GRANT TALKED ABOUT THE SERVICE THAT A LARGE 'PLANE COULD PROVIDE TO PROSPECTORS. HE GOT THE $55,000.00 AIRCRAFT FOR ONLY $2,500.00!

FIRST FLIGHT OVER THE ROCKIES . . .

A FLIGHT TO VANCOUVER OVER THE ROCKIES MADE HISTORY IN 1935. AT ONE POINT HOWEVER, THEY WERE FORCED TO TURN BACK BECAUSE OF ICE. THERE BEING NO RADIO CONTACT THEY WERE FEARED LOST. ON THE SECOND TRY GRANT FLEW LOW THROUGH THE WARMER VALLEYS - TO A HERO'S WELCOME!

ONCE, CAUGHT IN A "WHITE-OUT" NEAR EDMONTON, GRANT GOT HIS BEARINGS BY FLYING DOWN 99th STREET SO LOW THAT HE COULD SEE INTO OFFICE WINDOWS.

BY DESCRIBING A "FUTURE" ROUTE OVER THE TOP OF THE WORLD TO CHINA, AS A LOGICAL EXTENSION OF HIS YUKON SERVICE, GRANT PERSUADED THE DIRECTORS OF IMPERIAL OIL TO EXTEND $100,000.00 IN CREDIT - AT *NO INTEREST* . . .!

THE CHICAGO FIRE . . !

McCONACHIE'S "GREAT CHICAGO FIRE" WAS ANOTHER EXAMPLE OF HIS INCREDIBLE GOOD LUCK! AT TAKE-OFF GRANT'S 'PLANE CAUGHT FIRE AND ROARED AROUND IN EVER-INCREASING CIRCLES - JUST MISSING THE HUGE AIRLINERS ON THE AIRPORT. THE "FLEET-FREIGHTER" WAS A WRITE-OFF BUT IT HAD BEEN INSURED ONLY TWO HOURS EARLIER BY THE TWO INSURANCE EXECUTIVES WHO HAD COME TO SEE GRANT OFF. OF THE TWELVE AIRCRAFT HE OWNED AT THAT TIME THREE WERE LOST IN ACCIDENTS . . . . AND THEY WERE THE *ONLY* ONES THAT WERE COVERED BY INSURANCE.

FLYING BY CIGAR.! LEAVING EDMONTON AND IMMEDIATELY CLIMBING ABOVE THE CLOUDS, GRANT LIT A CIGAR AND, WHEN HE HAD SMOKED IT TO A CERTAIN LENGTH, HE WENT DOWN THROUGH THE CLOUD DECK AND, TO THE ASTONISHMENT OF HIS PASSENGER, THEY WERE OVER THEIR DESTINATION!

LANDING STRIPS WERE NECESSARY FOR THE "YUKON ROUTE" THAT GRANT HAD ORGANIZED. COMMUNITIES ENTHUSIASTICALLY CLEARED STRIPS AFTER GRANT HAD DESCRIBED THE PROSPERITY AND PRESTIGE THAT AIR SERVICE WOULD BRING.

YUKON AIR TRANSPORT WAS FORMED BY JOINING TEN "BUSH" LINES. C.P.R. THEN BOUGHT THIS NEW COMPANY AND 37-YEAR OLD GRANT McCONACHIE WAS NAMED PRESIDENT OF **CANADIAN PACIFIC AIRWAYS.**

THE CANADIAN TRADE COMMISSIONER NEGOTIATED FOR MONTHS TO GET A PERMIT FOR C.P.A. TO OPERATE TO AND FROM **AUSTRALIA...**

...BUT FAILED. IN *ONE* SPEACH AT A "FAREWELL" DINNER, GRANT CHANGED THE "FIRM" NEGATIVE DECISION OF THE AUSTRALIANS TO ONE OF ACCEPTANCE.

JAPAN WAS IMPORTANT IN C.P.A.'S PLANS TO EXPAND IN THE PACIFIC. AFTER MANY FRUSTRATING WEEKS OF WAITING GRANT GOT AN INTERVIEW WITH GENERAL MacARTHUR AND AFTER ONLY A FEW MINUTES HE CAME AWAY WITH THE PERMITS HE WANTED.

RELATIVES OF **CHINESE CANADIANS** WERE NOW ALLOWED INTO CANADA AND C.P.A. WAS THERE TO CARRY THEM FROM HONG KONG (THE ESCAPE ROUTE FROM CHINA). THEY AND AMERICAN SERVICEMEN BROUGHT PROSPERITY TO C.P.A.'S PACIFIC ADVENTURE.

GRANT FOUGHT GOVERNMENT REGULATION AND T.C.A. (AIR CANADA) MONOPOLY. HE SPOKE OFTEN OF THE VIRTUES OF INDIVIDUAL INITIATIVE AND PROVED HIS POINT BY TAKING ONLY EIGHT YEARS TO DEVELOP THE "BUSH ROUTES" INTO A MAJOR INTERNATIONAL AIR LINE.

BIG PHYSICALLY AND IN VISION AND IDEAS, GRANT HAD A CAPTIVATING PERSONALITY. HIS BOUNDLESS ENTHUSIASM AND IMAGINATION COMBINED WITH HIS ASTONISHMENT AT THE WORLD OF AVIATION TO BRING AN EXCITEMENT TO EVERYTHING HE UNDERTOOK. SURELY GRANT McCONACHIE DESERVES TO BE KNOWN AS A **CANADIAN GIANT!**

FOR THE COMPLETE STORY OF GRANT McCONACHIE READ "BUSH PILOT WITH A BRIEFCASE" BY RONALD A. KEITH, PUBLISHED BY DOUBLEDAY CANADA LIMITED IN 1972.

THE CAVES OF EUCLATAWS
by: Kathleen Lang

Stalactites in Euclataws hang down like folded drapes,
a myriad winter icicles in multi-forms and shapes;
a backdrop to the theatre stage of earth's deep awesome caves
as patiently the cavern floor the dripping water paves.

Stalagmites rear pillars high in Gothic columns tall,
and simulated ocean waves extend from wall to wall,
while helmet-lights reveal the sparks of diamond-spangled space —
ten thousand years of artistry give beauty to the place!

But I would see the frail design of fairy helictite
defying gravity, to hang a spelunker's delight;
"bacon strip" and "moon-milk" parquetry the floors
beneath the fragile helictites in lovely Euclataws.

Canada's Ten Longest and Deepest Caves

Longest

	Surveyed		Explored	
	Feet	Metres	Feet	Metres
1. Castleguard Cave, Alberta	43,000	13,100	Same	
2. Nakimu Caves, B.C.	19,000	5,790	19,500+	5,950+
3. Yorkshire Pot, B.C.	18,189	5,544	19,000+	5,800+
4. Gargantua, B.C.	17,277	5,260	18,000+	5,500+
5. Arctomys Cave, B.C.	7,927	2,414	9,000+	2,700+
6. Grotte Valerie, N.W.T.	6,233	1,900	Same	
7. Coral Cave, B.C.	4,774	1,455	Same	
8. Cascade Cave, B.C.	3,503	1,068	4,000+	1,200+
9. Grotte Mickey, N.W.T.	3,428	1,045	Same	
10. Moira Cave, Ontario	3,166	965	6,500+	2,000+

Deepest

	Feet	Metres
1. Arctomys Cave, B.C.	1,715	522
2. Yorkshire Pot, B.C.	1,260	384
3. Castleguard Cave, Alberta	1,018	310
4. Gargantua, B.C.	888	271
5. Nakimu Caves, B.C.	885	269
6. Chungo Cave, Alberta	425	130
7. Maquinna Cave, B.C.	356	109
8. Cascade Cave, B.C.	342	103
9. "D6", B.C.	331	101
10. Ice Hall, Alberta	318	97

The Big Room, Carlsbad Caverns

Great Caves of the World

by: Robert F. Nielsen

photos: U.S. Department of the Interior, British Travel Association,
Yugoslav National Tourist Office

Take one area of the earth which has an abundance of limestone. Add high mountains and deep valleys. Pour millions of tons of water over it for thousands upon thousands of years.

And there you have it; a simple recipe for deep caves! The water, converted to a weak acid by absorbing carbon dioxide from the soil, seeps through gaps in the earth's surface and dissolves the limestone below. When the water evaporates, it leaves holes in the earth, which eventually become enormous underground galleries. The world's great caves.

Europe

Alpine Europe, with all the ingredients for impressive caves, contains 44 of the 50 deepest in the world. France is especially fortunate, boasting the top four. *Gouffre de la Pierre St. Martin* is in the Pyrénées Mountains; a series of chambers ends in La Verna, a monstrous spherical vault 200 metres (650 feet) wide. Plunging to a great depth of 1332 metres (4370 feet), the Pierre St. Martin Cave is the world's deepest. Another impressive French cavern is *Gouffre Berger;* a string of massive galleries contains clusters of giant stalagmites on floors of pure white calcite.

Many European nations blessed with impressive caverns have converted them into "show caves," designed to delight tourists. Near Trieste, Italy, is *Grotta Gigante,* a single colossal "room" 125 metres (400 feet) high and long. A staircase aids the visitor in making the lengthy descent to a stalagmite-studded floor. One can tour Italy's *Postumia Grotto* with no effort at all; simply board the electric tram! Similarly, the stunning *Postojna Cave* in Yugoslavia — a cave-lover's paradise — has had a miniature railroad since 1872. The magnificence of Postojna is brilliantly displayed; there are paved pathways and bridges, and spectacular lighting effects. A major attraction is The Spaghetti Hall, aptly named for its ceiling, a mass of "sodastraw" stalactites. Close to Postojna is the gigantic mediaeval *Castle of Predjama,* built in the mouth of a cave. *Skocjan Cave,* also in Yugoslavia, is one of the wonders of the world; enormous floodlights reveal a fantastic underworld of wild precipitous gorges, magnificent river galleries, rapids, waterfalls and lakes.

Many thousands of visitors have thrilled to the great ice caves of Europe, especially *Eisriesenwelt* ("Ice Giant World") — the world's largest ice cave — in Austria, with its massive stalagmites and translucent curtains, all of crystal clear ice. The gaping entrance to Eisriesenwelt, high in the Alps, leads into a massive tunnel, its floors, walls and ceilings thick with ice. Forty

Postojna Cave, Yugoslavia

kilometres (25 miles) of galleries include The Castle of the Gods, a chamber of thick ice walls containing blood-red streaks which glow like flames, and Ice Gate, its transparent walls replete with ice bubbles resembling bunches of luscious grapes. Utgarsburg, a great vaulted-roof chamber, leads into Alexander Mork's Cathedral, the largest room in the cave, where — in a marble urn atop a marble altar — are the ashes of Mork, a famous cave explorer. There are other impressive subterranean palaces of ice: *Dachstein Cave,* also in Austria, *Demanova* in Czechoslovakia, *Schellenberg* in the German Alps, and *Balaganskaya* near Lake Baykal in Russia. (The Russians chose an appropriately long name for another of their caves — *Peschtschera Optimititscheskaja* is a maze of a hundred kilometres of passages, ranking it third longest on earth.)

Two European caves are renowned the world over for superb Palaeolithic paintings. The walls and ceilings of *Lascaux Cave* in France and *Altamira Cave* in Spain were enriched by hunters of the Old Stone Age, who used damp powdered stones as pigment to render lifelike animals: horses, boars, reindeer, bulls, bison . . . Why these magnificent works were created remains a mystery, although a likely theory holds that the artists believed if they could accurately portray their quarry, they would have success in the hunt. (See "The Painted Caves of Altamira," *Canadian Children's Annual 1978.*)

Great Britain

The British Isles do not have deep caves; nevertheless they have many, plus an abundance of eager cave explorers ("potholers"). The Yorkshire Downs are a major caving area, boasting *Gaping Gill Hole;* a single drop of 110 metres (360 feet) opens into the roof of the largest underground chamber in Britain, 150 metres (490 feet) long and 35 metres (115 feet) high. In the southwest are the Mendip Hills, containing the famous show cave *Wookey Hole,* the first cave in the world to be floodlit. Like the Russians, the British chose a long name for their longest cave — *Ogof Ffynnon Ddu* stretches 38 kilometres (24 miles) beneath the surface of south Wales.

Asia

Many of the major Asian caves have been converted into shrines and temples. The famous *Ajanta Caves* in India — a row of 29 caverns along the face of a cliff — have been deepened by man, who also added hefty pillars to guard entrances, and colourful murals to decorate walls. A magnificent sweep of steps leads to a trio of blue and gold pillars on the threshold of the *Batu Temple Cave* in Malaysia.

Japan has a beautiful show cave in *Akiyoshi-do.* The 10 kilometres (6 miles) of galleries include a series of lovely curving dams of calcite, each holding a pool of clear water.

Down Under

Both Australia and New Zealand have spectacular caves. Tasmania is a speleological hotbed, and southwestern Australia boasts *Jewel Cave* and *Strong's Cave,* rich with

Predjama Castle, Yugoslavia

the process of formation) open to public viewing. Here are thundering subterranean waterfalls, lofty ceilings and another awe-inspiring glow-worm grotto.

Mexico

Mexico has ideal conditions for caves, combining huge rivers and limestone aplenty with high mountains and a tropical climate. Here lies the deepest cave in North America — *Sotano de San Augustin,* 612 metres (2009 feet) in depth. Most unusual are Mexico's *cenotes,* enormous craters partially filled with water. Found in Yucatan, the most famous is the sacred well of the ancient city of Chichén Itzà. It was put to questionable use by the Mayan priests who, considering the enormous abyss an ideal place to offer sacrifices, threw young men and women to watery deaths.

The United States

Approximately 130 American caves are open to the public. One of the most famous is aptly named *Mark Twain Cave.* Near Hannibal, Missouri, its tortuous passages provided an ideal setting for the exciting pursuit of Tom Sawyer and Becky Thatcher by the surly Injun Joe. (See "A Day with Tom and Huck," *Canadian Children's Annual 1975.*)

But it is for two truly great caves that the United States is renowned in caving circles. *Mammoth Cave* in Kentucky is part of the *Flint-Mammoth Cave System* which, measuring an incredible 290 kilometres (180 miles), makes it easily the longest cave in the world. Each year thousands of tourists are led through a fraction of the lengthy passages — on walks which last up to six hours — to enjoy such phenomena as The Onyx Chamber, Mammoth Dome, and Frozen Niagara, a magnificent sheet of flowstone 23

inverted forests of "sodastraw" stalactites. A single "straw" in the latter betters 7 metres (25 feet) in length; it's probably the world's longest. Beneath the vast Nullarbor Plain is *Mullamullang Cave;* 10 kilometres (6 miles) long, its main tunnel resembles a gigantic subway.

The *Waitomo Caves* constitute one of New Zealand's major tourist haunts. Within the caves is the world-famous "Glow-worm Grotto"; visitors are transported via boat along an underground river to the cathedral-sized chamber. Provided everybody remains perfectly silent, they will see a sight of indescribable beauty; millions of glow-worms light the ceiling with a soft, eerie blue-green luminescence.

Waitomo is on North Island; South Island too has very special caves. Six of them in the Takaka-Mount Arthur region exceed 245 metres (800 feet) in depth. *Te-Anau-au* (a Maori word meaning "cave of rushing waters") is a rare specimen; one of the few "living" caves (i.e. still in

Wookey Hole, Somerset, England

metres (75 feet) high and 15 metres (50 feet) wide. Many visitors break for lunch in the Snowball Room, a restaurant with a natural ceiling of clusters of gypsum, located 80 metres (267 feet) beneath the earth's surface!

In 1925 a tragic accident focused world-wide attention on the Mammoth Cave area. Floyd Collins, a local cave explorer, was trapped in nearby *Sand Cave* when a rock dislodged from the ceiling and fell on his foot. Although at first his plight did not seem insurmountable, as day followed day the situation grew progressively desperate. Later Floyd's stepmother would tell of his premonition: "I been a-dreamin' of bein' caught in some rocks and some men a-clawin' at me." And Collins told a reporter who visited him in the mine that he had dreamed that angels riding white horses brought him white chicken sandwiches.

There were numerous theories about how to save Floyd Collins, but nothing worked. Quickly his problem caught the interest of the public and soon millions were following Collins' fate on radio and in newspapers. Outside Sand Cave was a veritable circus, as self-seekers of every description flooded the area to exploit a rapidly growing mob. Fast-food merchants sold hamburgers for twenty-five cents, five times the going rate. There were souvenir peddlers, jugglers, preachers, medicine men . . . Even Collins' own father wandered amongst the crowd distributing handbills advertising *Crystal Cave,* a family enterprise and another part of the Flint-Mammoth system. Scores of women offered to marry Collins; one wanted to march right into the cave dragging a preacher!

A week after Collins was trapped a digging party began tunnelling to him from the surface. For eleven days they dug, reaching Collins on the seventeenth day of his im-

prisonment. He was dead. On that day, 50,000 people were milling about the entrance to the cave!

Although Floyd Collins travelled not at all during the last two weeks of his life, in death he made up for it! Initially it was decided to leave the body in Sand Cave, but plans were altered; his corpse was removed and buried on a hillside near the mouth of Crystal Cave. Two years later ownership of the cave passed from the Collins family; the new proprietor had Floyd's body exhumed and put on display in a glass-topped coffin in the cave! Floyd stayed put for two years, but returned to his wandering ways when his body was stolen and thrown from a cliff into a nearby river. At least, that had been the intention of the thieves. Actually the body ended its flight in a tree, from which — minus one leg — it was retrieved. Floyd was returned to Crystal Cave, and he can be visited there today — although his glass-topped casket has been replaced by a less revealing receptacle. His tombstone briefly tells his story, and ends "Greatest Cave Explorer Ever Known."

Not everybody believes the incredible story of Floyd Collins. Recently one old-timer who lives near Mammoth Cave told a visiting reporter: "Don't you pay no attention to any of 'em, Floyd Collins ain't dead at all. They done it to get these here caves in the newspapers. It was just a dummy they took out of that sinkhole. Floyd's living on a ranch out in Arizona."

Amongst the 66 caves which constitute the fabulous *Carlsbad Caverns* in New Mexico is The Big Room. The largest underground chamber in the world, it exceeds a half mile in length, covers an area equal to 14 football fields, and has enough height to accommodate the U.S. Capitol building in one corner! Many of the 800,000 guests attracted by Carlsbad

Hall of Giants, Carlsbad Caverns

Giant & Twin Domes, Carlsbad Caverns

Bat Flight, Carlsbad Caverns

Caverns each year take a walk to The Big Room; it is a lengthy jaunt over enormous rock formations and through gigantic rooms, but the descent is gradual. Then the visitor enjoys a four-hour stroll around the 2 kilometre (1 1/4 mile) perimeter of The Big Room. (Less energetic cave-lovers can take an elevator to and from the room.)

Not surprisingly, Carlsbad contains many massive *speleothems* (cave formations): in addition to the usual *stalactites, stalagmites,* and *stalactostalagmites* (usually called "columns," and formed by the union of stalactite and stalagmite), there are huge domes. The Giant Dome is 19 metres (62 feet) high, and is similar in appearance to the Leaning Tower of Pisa.

The early evening sojourner at Carlsbad is in for a special treat; thousands of Mexican freetail bats spend the daylight hours in Bat Cave, the uppermost cavern, but when the light dissipates the tiny mammals spiral from the mouth of the cave. As they emerge — to enjoy an evening dining on flying insects — they form a black cloud of bodies which sweeps southward into the night sky.

A hunter once discovered a major U.S. cave when he heard whistling. Upon in-

The Totem Pole, Carlsbad Caverns

spection, he found that the source of the noise was a tiny entrance to a cave; the action of wind currents within had caused the sound. Common sense must have dictated the naming of *Wind Cave*, South Dakota. The same applies to neighbouring *Jewel Cave* — its walls are lined with sparkling calcite crystals — which ranks as the second longest cave in the U.S. with 83 kilometres (52 miles) of galleries.

And Many, Many More . . .

There are great caves in many other countries — Jamaica, Cuba, Venezuela, China, South Africa, and, of course, Canada — each offering a unique adventure to the visitor. During your travels, if you find yourself close to one of the fabulous show caves of the world, take the time to visit.

But remember to be extremely careful in a cave — take care not to deface irreplaceable cave formations, and — above all — avoid damage to something else irreplaceable — you!

And if you find yourself — alone — in a deep, dank, dark cave, try not to let your imagination get the better of you . . .

Crystal Spring Dome, Carlsbad Caverns

How To Use A Carbide Lamp

by: E.A. Carruthers   *illustrations: Ian Carr*

You're in a cave, halfway up a crack in the rock, with a brisk little waterfall splashing down over you. The rest of the party is waiting below. Your only light comes from the carbide lamp fixed to your helmet. As you climb, before you move hand or foot, you scan the wet rock with your beam, looking for some ledge that looks solid, for some slippery projection that won't come away in your grasp. The next hold you see is higher than usual, and for a minute you forget, and look up too high. The falling water douses your light. You are left in utter darkness, unable to see your hands, your feet, the cold rock all around and far below, or the water that got you into this predicament.

* * * * * *

To explore a world of darkness, you must bring your own light with you. You must also know what light to bring. Occasional beginners venture into a cave with a hand-held candle or flashlight. They do not get far or last long. In a cave you need both hands free for climbing; and flashlight batteries soon grow dim. The caver's standard lamp is a small, light-weight

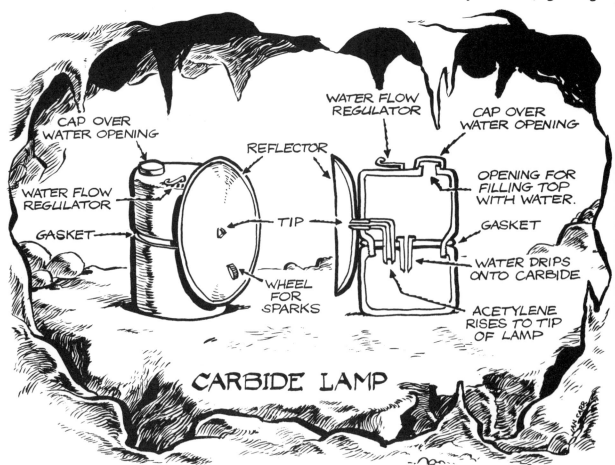

CARBIDE LAMP

- CAP OVER WATER OPENING
- WATER FLOW REGULATOR
- GASKET
- REFLECTOR
- TIP
- WHEEL FOR SPARKS
- WATER FLOW REGULATOR
- CAP OVER WATER OPENING
- OPENING FOR FILLING TOP WITH WATER.
- GASKET
- WATER DRIPS ONTO CARBIDE
- ACETYLENE RISES TO TIP OF LAMP

carbide lamp attached to the front of a miner's helmet. In that position it shines where the wearer looks, and it leaves both hands free.

The principle of the carbide lamp is simple. It burns acetylene, a highly combustible gas which it generates as required by adding water at a controlled rate to calcium carbide. You thus do not have to carry along a heavy cylinder of inflammable gas, but only small amounts of the required calcium carbide and water. (An eight-ounce bottle of carbide will provide light for six to eight hours.)

To use the lamp, fill the bottom about two-thirds full of calcium carbide. Separately fill the top with water. Clean the tip with the fine wire tool you carry for the purpose — it comes with the lamp — and adjust the water regulator so that the water drips at about a drop per second. Be sure the gasket is in place, and screw the top securely to the bottom. Water is now dripping steadily onto the calcium carbide, creating acetylene and calcium hydroxide (slaked lime, or "spent carbide"). The acetylene begins to escape through the tip. To know when a steady flow is established, listen to it hiss, or hold a wet finger in the stream of gas. If there's only a weak gas flow, clean the tip again and increase the water flow-rate slightly. When the gas is flowing steadily, you're ready to light the lamp.

Lighting the lamp is easy, especially if you have big hands. (Of course, you could use a match or a companion's lamp, but that does not teach you how to light a lamp when all the matches are wet and everyone's lamp is out.) Holding the lamp in the left hand, cup your right palm for a few seconds over the reflector. During those few seconds a small pocket of acetylene accumulates between your hand and the reflector. If you have small hands, choose a brand of lamp with a small reflector. It is essential to be able to cover the reflector with your palm.

After that short pause, move your right hand briskly down and off the reflector, using a wiping motion, so that the moving palm turns the little steel wheel of the sparking device. The spark mechanism is the same as that of a cigarette lighter. The steel strikes a spark from the flint, the spark ignites the jet of acetylene, and suddenly you can see again. Adjust the water rate as needed to control the size of your flame.

A few tips. First, carry spares: a couple of extra tips, since these are only pressed in place and can fall out; a couple of flints; a spare gasket, since that sometimes falls off when you dump the spent carbide; and twice as much carbide as you expect to need.

Never forget to take your tip-cleaner, and clean the tip with every fill. There's usually a particle of soot or spent carbide half-plugging the opening.

It's smart to practice taking your lamp apart above ground, while blindfolded. Empty the spent carbide, take the lamp apart (remembering by touch where all the pieces are), clean it thoroughly, fill, reassemble, and light, all with a blindfold on. Above ground, the mistakes you make the first few times won't matter.

Your carbide bottle must be watertight and unbreakable. A plastic, screw-top bottle ideal for the purpose may often be found cheaply at cosmetic counters, in the bin with plastic soapdishes for travel, and the like.

Carry a plastic bag for spent carbide, and take that, with any other garbage, with you when you leave the cave.

When rappelling into a pit on a rope (a skill to be learned from experts and practiced first on a gentle slope above ground), never look directly at the rope. If you do, you play your flame directly on the rope, just above your hands. Hemp will burn, and nylon will melt. Neither is good for your caving career.

You cannot strike a spark from wet flint and steel. Consequently, you cannot light your lamp with a wet hand. If you are only moderately wet yourself, you may be able to dry your hand on some inner layer of clothing. Finding a dry layer becomes increasingly difficult in some caves and may become impossible if, for instance, your light goes out while you are climbing through a waterfall. (The last dry spot on your person, oddly enough, is likely to be your armpit.) It is good to carry, in your kit of spares, a few matches in a completely watertight container. Do not forget to include something dry in the container to strike them on. Wet rocks or the sole of your sodden boot will not serve.

And if your light does go out while you are still hanging onto that cliff under the waterfall? Easy. Just switch on your electric light. It's mounted on your helmet, too: the bulb and reflector in front and the batteries in a small metal box on the back, for balance. It won't last long: only two or three hours before the batteries fail. But that's long enough to get you up a dozen waterfalls. After all, no good caver would go underground with only one lighting system.

Canada's Rocky Mountain Subway

by: Robert F. Nielsen
Photos: Dr. Derek Ford,
Department of Geology, McMaster University

Exhausted by their ordeal, the two young men moved painstakingly forward. Suddenly — unexpectedly — they encountered danger; when they entered the cave many hours before, the floor had been dry. Now it was submerged, and with every step the water grew deeper. To escape, however, they must continue their descent, because this had been a most unusual cave; exploration had necessitated a gradual climb, instead of the usual plunge into the depths. And since only one entrance had been found, the caver must leave by the same route he entered. Soon the water was up to their necks; another step forward would have been suicidal.

They were trapped!

So this was the price to be paid for disturbing the sanctity of Castleguard, Canada's longest and most magnificent cave!

Afraid that the water might continue to rise, the men retreated to a spot where they had left some supplies, anticipating a return visit. They had not expected to be back so soon! Numbed by the cold, they tried to dry their clothes with heat from carbide lamps, normally used to light their way. Then they dug a shallow depression in the sandy floor, where they huddled together for warmth, their sodden bodies wracked with spasms of shivering.

"It's ruddy cold in here."

"So it is. Cuddle closer."

"Have we anything to eat?"

"Only some dehydrated soup, but no cooking pot."

"Could we use a helmet and a carbide lamp?"

"No. There's no carbide left."

Fortunately the water soon began to subside, and a rescue team appeared. They immediately congratulated the two men for having just made history; the first persons ever to have trekked the eight miles to the end of Castleguard and back.

Well, almost to the end! Three years later — in 1970 — Boon returned to the cave and performed one of the most stunning feats of derring-do ever recorded; he explored the entire length of Castleguard entirely on his own! At a juncture known as The Crutch deep within the cave Boon took the left fork rather than the right, his and Thompson's previous choice. As he pressed relentlessly forward, Boon was halted in his tracks by a brilliant blast of reflected light. It emanated from a glittering wall of ice which completely blocked the passage. Boon was 13.1 kilometres (8.2 miles) from the entrance of Castleguard, and he had just discovered the "exit," right at the bottom of the Columbia Icefield, the surface of which was a thousand feet above!

A dozen years ago Canada was

considered destitute of impressive caves, a notion which has been altered — drastically — due to the efforts of a host of *spelunkers* (cave explorers) and *speleologists* (cave scientists). These men and women have discovered and explored several enormous caverns, some of which rank amongst the world's longest and deepest. Most of them are located in the Rocky Mountains.

Castleguard Cave is the most impressive of them all. Not only one of the largest caves in the world, it is also one of the most interesting. Castleguard actually tunnels its way clean through a mountain — Mount Castleguard in Jasper Park. Although its existence has been known for fifty years, it was not until the last decade that it was systematically explored and surveyed.

Castleguard offers to the caver superb examples of most of the phenomena associated with caves. There is a perfect example of a *phreatic tube,* a passage formed by the pressure of water pushing its way through an opening in the rock. The Subway, as the tube is appropriately called, is a circular passage four metres in diameter. Often compared to an enormous gun barrel, The Subway runs dead straight for 300 metres. Beyond The Subway lie First Fissure and Second Fissure, which demonstrate another type of passage, the *vadose canyon,* caused by water which has a gravitational flow, with air space above it. A combination of a phreatic tube and a vadose canyon produces a *keyhole passage,* such as the Holes-in-the-Floor.

Halfway along the length of Castleguard is an area called The Grottoes; here the caver finds a fantastic collection of *speleothems,* or calcite cave deposits. There are *"straws,"* thin *stalactites* hollow in the centre; *helictites,* crazily shaped projections which grow from the walls; *flowstones,* softly contoured formations which cover walls and floors; and nests of perfectly formed *cave pearls,* up to an inch in diameter, created by water drops falling into pools of saturated water and depositing their calcium around minute particles of sand. (Another similar phenomenon is *cave popcorn,* small clusters of rounded calcium deposits.)

Although it is Canada's longest cavern, Castleguard is not its deepest. This honour falls to Arctomys Cave. With its entrance high on the slopes of Mount Robson, Arctomys consists of a seemingly endless series of tiny waterfalls which carry a thin stream to the great depth of 522 metres (1715 feet). Not a deeper cave exists in either Canada or the United States.

Other spectacular caves in the Rockies include Gargantua, so named because of a network of huge tunnels, and Yorkshire Pot, its series of vertical shafts leading down to an extensive network of phreatic tubes, including The Roller Coaster Run (so named because of its many twists and turns, ups and downs) and The Horror Show (Its walls are coated with thick mud!). In the Crowsnest Pass is a cave with a stunningly beautiful name — The Glittering Ice Palace; when illuminated by the cavers' lamps, its ice-floored, crystal-walled chamber magically glistens and gleams. Other fine ice caves are at Plateau Mountain — its walls and ceilings are thick with layers of perfectly formed hexagonal crystals — and at Nahanni River in the Northwest Territories.

The Nakimu Caves in Glacier National Park were a major tourist attraction for many years. Guests of the Glacier House, a nearby hotel, journeyed to the caves and, equipped with carbide lamps, descended a series of wooden staircases. Some brave souls, dangling from a knotted rope, lowered themselves into The Gorge. In 1909 Nakimu hosted more than a thousand visitors; in 1917 a stage coach was

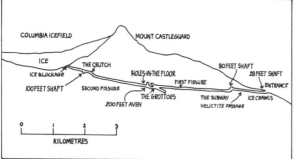

damages. Recently there were reports of "a mysterious cave in the Gaspe Peninsula which has a 40-foot pit full of the bones of people and animals who have wandered in over centuries." There are about a hundred good-sized caves in Ontario, most of them confined to the line of cliffs which forms the Niagara Escarpment. Two Ontario caves are flourishing commercial enterprises: Scenic Caves near Collingwood, and Bonnechere Cave outside Eganville. The longest cave in eastern Canada — Moira Cave, north of Belleville — is in Ontario.

But the prize for Best Canadian Cave must be reserved for Castleguard. A round-trip visit to its end is considered one of the most exciting — and demanding — caving experiences in the world. The adventure — reserved only for experts — takes four days; four days of gruelling physical labour. Anyone prepared for a casual eight mile hike in the dark is in for a nasty shock; he will find himself crawling flat-out along floors of ice, descending a skimpy ladder twenty-five metres into a black abyss, wading waist-deep through pools of frigid water, and, along Holes-in-the-Floor, testing his "wall of death" technique. (This consists of running so quickly around the top of a deep pit that the caver's centrifugal force keeps him from tumbling into its depths!)

So impressive is Castleguard that a movie was made about it. Called simply "Castleguard Cave," it records the adventures of five speleologists, led by Dr. Derek Ford of McMaster University, on an expedition into the cave. Making the movie proved a formidable task; teams of cavers had to carry camera and lighting gear far into the depths of the cave. But it was worth it; "Castleguard Cave" provides a fascinating and enlightening look at the world of caves and cavers. It reveals the extreme physical and mental stamina as well as the mountain-goat like agility required by the cave explorer. It demonstrates the necessity for highly specialized equipment if one intends to travel in caves as demanding as this one. Above all, the film proves the need for extreme safety precautions; an injury which might be considered minor under normal conditions could prove fatal if suffered miles inside a mountain.

There is a world of caves, and each cave is a world unto itself. Canada has been blessed with an abundance of these subterranean worlds to explore — and to protect. Although some of them have already been found, Canada's cave hunters suspect that many more remain undiscovered, each one a keeper of strange and fascinating mysteries.

introduced to carry tourists from the hotel along "Tally-Ho Road" to the caves. All activity stopped in 1935, following the closing of Glacier House, but plans are afoot to reopen the caves to visitors.

Not all of Canada's caves are in the Rockies. Vancouver Island has a host of impressive examples, and *spelunking* is a popular pastime. The Vancouver Island Cave Exploration Group even publishes a bulletin; "Cave Notes" implores its members to:

Take Nothing But Photographs
Leave Nothing But Footprints
Kill Nothing But Time.

Amongst the hundreds of caverns which have been explored, two of the most popular are Cascade Cave — also known as Hobbit Hole — and Euclataws. The latter demonstrates how imaginative cavers are when they name the parts of a cave; in one small area are: "The Witches' Ballroom," "The Meatgrinder," "Organpipe Gallery," "Diving Board Aven," "The Attic," "The Basement," and "The Dome Room."

There are a few notable caves in eastern Canada. One of the best-known is Howes Cave near Saint John, New Brunswick, the subject of many local legends about its contents (although one resident was quoted as saying "I was never able to find anything but bats and slime"). Quebec has numerous caves, notably Caverne Lafleche, in Gatineau County, open to the public for fifty years but closed due to

Pothole

by: E.A. Carruthers   illustrations: Ian Carr

Only an incident, but it nearly finished my caving. It happened last trip, a week ago. There were four of us in the party, a good number for a long trip — and a good group, too. We'd been out before and worked well together.

The cave had been known for a couple of years and was fairly thoroughly explored. We were going mainly as tourists, but, since I was there, we planned to have a look at a small lead that no one else had been able to push. I'm considered useful for small leads. Sometimes the others call me "the club ferret."

It was a good cave, a "friendly cave," as Tim put it: clean and open, easy going for the most part, with enough vertical bits to keep Bill reasonably cheerful, if not actually satisfied.

We took about five hours to get to the lead, a hole about four feet up in the left-hand wall, a trifle higher than it was wide. Side entry. No question. That hole looked about big enough to admit my cat. Otherwise, though, it looked good: a solution tube through the wall that might go a long way before it pinched out. Or before it opened out into some "cavern measureless to man," those awesome chambers and endless passages we all dreamed about, however little we might admit it, because we all knew that in sober fact they might be there, just around the next bend. Others have made such discoveries. Why not ourselves, this trip, or maybe the next one?

The tangible passage before us pierced the wall for at least twenty feet before it curved to the left out of sight. On closer inspection, it looked a trifle bigger. One or another of the smaller cavers might even have been able to enter it — but, of course, the trip was bound to be easier for me.

Tim gave me a lift in — it was rather like feeding a shell into a cannon — and I settled down to the familiar discomforts. If a passage is too narrow for your shoulders, you traverse it on one side. If it's a bit narrower still, your hard-hat comes off, because the brim is too wide, and you push it ahead of you for the light.

If the roof is high, you're reasonably comfortable: you progress by pushing against high projections on the wall with your feet and hauling with your hands. If the roof is low, the arm beneath you stretches forward along the passage floor ahead of you, and the other arm trails backward along your body. Shoulders aslant are not so high. In such a passage — and this was such a passage — there's no width in which to bend your knees for leverage, no height to reach a foot into for a hold. In such a passage you move with your toes, with your ribs, like a snake, and with your leading arm, which is pushing your hard-hat for the light, and aches.

I entered on my right side, since that arm is the stronger, and on that side I stayed. There was no room to turn over. At least the passage was straight. I'd been in others that looped like a mountain road or a lowland creek. This one had a few minor bends, but nothing to cause trouble.

Some distance in I stopped to consider and to get my breath. I was very hot by then, a little tired, and beginning to get fed up. Why couldn't the thing make up its mind? If it wasn't going to come out into something big, then it ought to pinch out completely. No need to go on and on like this. Still, there was another bend ahead, and perhaps the answer was just around that one.

It was. But it was no answer I'd ever considered.

I waited until I'd caught my breath and cooled off again, in reasonable comfort. The space had increased slightly, and I was even able to put my hard-hat back on. Finally I started on again.

It was a slow business. I was on my right side still, right arm extended forward and getting tired, left arm backward. There's a certain pride in being able to go where no one else can; but occasionally I consider, when tired, that where no one can follow, no one can rescue. My arm ached, and suddenly I wanted the passage to get bigger.

The bend, a left-hand one this time, was no worse than its predecessors, and it looked like most of them. I was about halfway around, almost enough to see the next stretch of passage, when my right hand, which I could not see, closed on something that was neither rock nor mud. It was nothing living, but I let it go as one does a spider picked up unexpectedly, and lurched forward to see.

It had been another caver once, long ago, like myself, stretched out in that narrow passage in a position that was the mirror image of my own, and what I had grasped in my outstretched leading hand were the bones of his.

I backed out of that passage faster than I would normally have believed possible and landed back among the others — the swearing, complaining, blessed, living others — with an impetuousness for which I was rebuked. Charlie has never encouraged people to step on him, and my boots are nailed. I must have looked something of what I felt, for the comments, pithily begun, ended abruptly. I reported, coolly, I thought, under the circumstances, and for a while we thought our own thoughts.

I sat where I'd landed and gradually, of course, calmed down. And that was bad, because I forgot some of the horror and became curious. After all, were bones so dreadful? It was just coming on them so suddenly. We'd brought a camera along. Surely we ought to get some pictures. The others thought me mad, but why not? So I got out the camera, set it up — there would be no room to do so there — and started back.

It had been a hard journey the first time, and it was far harder the second, wearied and encumbered as I was. I had to stop several times for breath and to ease my aching arm. I recognized the bend at once, and nearly changed my mind. But it was not possible to go so far and then to go back to the others and say, "I went so far and could not."

Indeed, when I got around the bend again, it was not so horrible as before. It was just bones, stretched out in a narrow passage.

I took pictures as well as I could, but one-handed photography is not easy, especially changing bulbs, and I was glad to finish and rest a while again, almost against his arm, our skulls hardly separated in the little space.

And only then did I begin to think. The initial shock must have been worse than I'd realized. Why was he here? Why had he died in a passage which I knew to be clear ahead of him? Water? A flash flood? And then I saw it. I had taken half a dozen pictures that would show it, but not until now did I see it. His legs. They were hidden from the knees down, buried in a mass of half-compacted mud and stone that had slipped

quietly out of the roof behind him as he crawled, how long ago? to hold him there forever.

I thought of the long trail behind me back to life, its roof already thrice disturbed by my passage. I thought of two cavers, indeed the mirror images of each other, white skull reflecting skull, arms reaching out, white ribs and back and legs and dead brown rock, each facing each, forever. And then I knew horror.

* * * * * *

Yes, I got out all right. You knew that, of course. How else would I be telling you all this? And I'll go caving again. There's a trip planned for next weekend, a nice, big vertical cave. I'll probably try the little cracks again, too, for there's a lure about going where no one can follow that's hard to resist. But not yet awhile.

ALIEN WORLDS PROBE: SERIES #3

SOMEWHERE AROUND HERE.

PLANET: #351 A, M 101 GALAXY... DISTANCE FROM EARTH: 12 MILLION LIGHT YEARS... NO. OF PLANETS IN SOLAR SYSTEM: ONE... MEAN DIS. FROM SUN: 36 MILLION MILES... MEAN DIA.: 3.5 THOUSAND (EARTH) MILES... REVOLVES AROUND SUN: 135 DAYS... AXIAL ROTATION: 13½ HRS.,... MASS (EARTH =1): 0.35... AVERAGE SURFACE TEMP.: 110° F. AT EQUATOR. TEMP. DROPS TO 95° F. AT N. AND S. POLES.

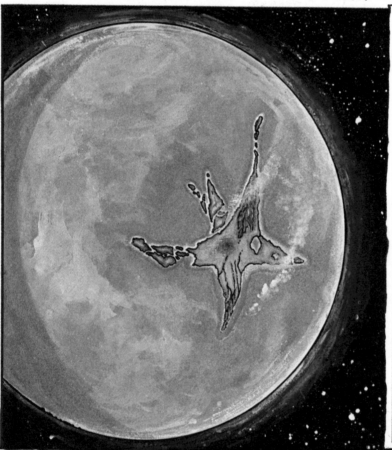

THE PLANET FOR THE MOST PART IS COVERED BY WATER EXCEPT FOR ONE STAR-SHAPED CLUSTER OF ISLANDS. FIVE DISTINCT GEOGRAPHICAL REGIONS MAKE UP THESE ISLANDS: THE ROCKY AND DESOLATE NORTH SHORE (INCLUDING THE CENTRAL DESERT ZONE); THE NORTH EASTERN HIGHLANDS WITH ITS TOWERING GRELB MT. RANGE; THE TROPICAL AND FERTILE WESTERN ISLANDS; THE SWAMPY SOUTH-WESTERN SPIKE, WITH ITS HUNDREDS OF RIVERS AND STREAMS; AND THE SOUTH-EASTERN FLATLANDS WHICH END AT THE SEA IN LONG ORANGE-COLORED BEACHES.

EACH SEPARATE GEOGRAPHICAL REGION ON THE PLANET SERVES AS HOME FOR FIVE DISTINCT FORMS OF LIFE. THESE LIFE FORMS ARE INTELLIGENT AND SHARE A COMMON LANGUAGE. THE NAME THE LAND IS COMMONLY KNOWN AS IS "CRITJ" (PRO: "KREE J"), WHICH TRANSLATED ROUGHLY MEANS "THIS HERE PLACE THAT WHICH WE ARE ON."

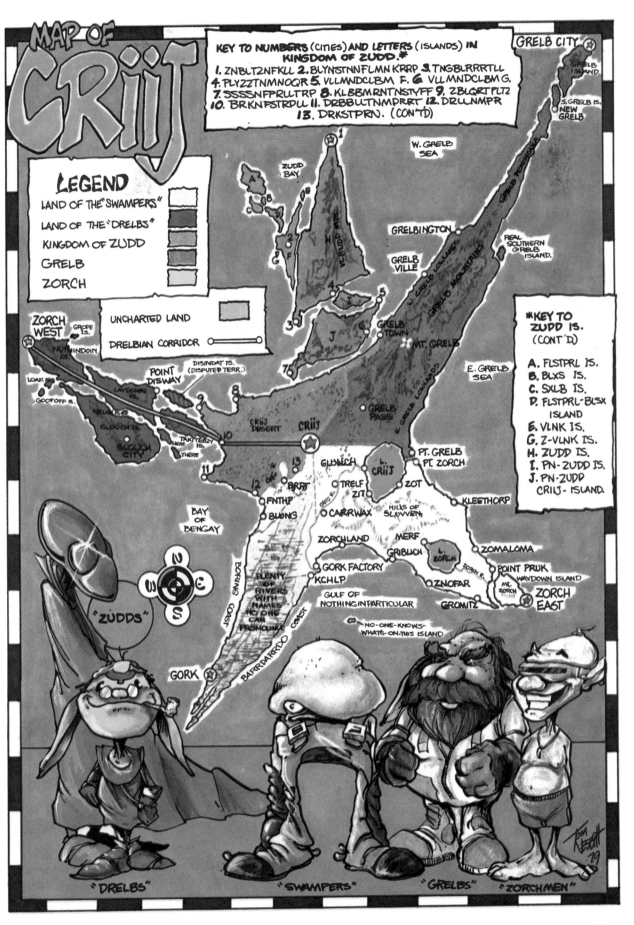

123

THE DIMINUTIVE, RABBIT-EARED DRELBS INHABIT THE NORTH-WESTERN ISLANDS OF CRIIJ. THESE TROPICAL ISLES ARE PERFECT FOR THE EASY-GOING DRELB LIFESTYLE. HUNTING AND FISHING ARE MAJOR ACTIVITIES OF THE DRELBS. THEY SELDOM LEAVE THEIR ISLANDS EXCEPT TO TRADE AT THE MARKET IN CRIIJ CITY. THEIR ONE AND ONLY EXPORT IS A YELLOW AND BLUE PLANT CALLED "STUPHF."

THE HUSKY, BEARDED GRELBS ARE THE MINERS, FARMERS AND LABOURERS OF CRIIJ. DISTANT RELATIVES TO THE DRELBS, MOST GRELBS CONSIDER THEM LAY-ABOUTS AND BUMS. HOWEVER, THE DRELB ARE NEEDED FOR THEIR "STUPHF" WHICH IS AN IMPORTANT INGREDIENT TO THE GRELB DIET AND MAKES WORK UNDER THE TORRID CRIIJIAN SUN TOLERABLE.

LIFE ON CRiiJ

THE MYSTERIOUS, WARLIKE ZUDDS INHABIT THE DESO-LATE, ARRID NORTH-ERN SPIKE. LITTLE IS KNOWN OF THESE ARMOR-CLAD PEO-PLE (NO ONE HAS EVER SEEN ONE WITH HIS CLOTHES OFF.) EXCEPT THAT THEY STAND IN ONE PLACE WITHOUT MOV-ING A LOT AND THEIR LANGUAGE IS TOT-ALLY CONFUSING.

Tom Nebbit 79

THE GOLDEN-SKINNED ZORCH-MEN OF ZORCH ARE INDEED A PECULIAR RACE. ABOUT THE ONLY THINGS THEY CAN DO IS RUN BEACH RESORTS AND HOTELS. SO THAT'S WHAT THEY DO. ZORCH HAS THE MOST CITIES, HIGH-WAYS, HOTELS, MOTELS, INNS & BARS IN ALL OF CRIIJ. IT ALSO HAS THE HIGHEST POPULATION (MOSTLY OUT-OF-TOWNERS).

THE GROTESQUE LOOKING SWAMPERS ARE AT THE BOTTOM OF THE SOCIAL AND ECO-NOMIC SCALE IN CRIIJ. ALL OTHER INHABITANTS CONSIDER THEM ANTISOCIAL, SMELLY, RUDE, CLUMSY, BORING AND GOOD ONLY FOR CATCHING THE DISGUST-ING LOOKING SEA CREATURES THAT THEY SELL. ALL THIS IS ABSOLUTELY TRUE.

THE CITY OF CRIIJ IS THE MAJOR TRADING AND CULTURAL CENTRE OF CRIIJ. IT IS HERE THAT THE FIVE MAJOR TRIBES OF THE ISLANDS COME TOGETHER AND LIVE IN HARMONY (OR AT LEAST TOLERATE ONE ANOTHER), LOCATED IN THE CENTRE OF THE CRIIJ DESERT. THE BORDERS OF ALL THE KINGDOMS DISSECT THE CITY INTO FIVE SEPARATE SECTIONS, WHICH FALL UNDER THE JURISDICTION OF THEIR RESPECTIVE GOVERNMENTS. THE DRELBS, WHO HAVE NO CLAIM TO ANY AREA OF THE MAINLAND, HAVE ACCESS TO CRIIJ THROUGH THE "DRELBIAN CORRIDOR", A TREACHEROUS "HIGHWAY ON STILTS" WHICH STRETCHES FROM "ZORCH WEST" THROUGH ZUDD TERRITORY AND INTO THE CITY. THE ZUDDS, NEEDLESS TO SAY, ARE NOT TOO PLEASED. CRIIJ, INCIDENTLY, IS BUILT ON TOP OF AN EXTINCT VOLCANO CRATER, AND IS EXPECTED AT SOME POINT TO BE BLOWN OFF THE FACE OF THE PLANET. SINCE CRIIJ IS CONSIDERED "NEUTRAL", VIOLENCE WITHIN THE CITY IS STRICTLY FORBIDDEN, AND LAWS ARE STRICTLY ENFORCED.

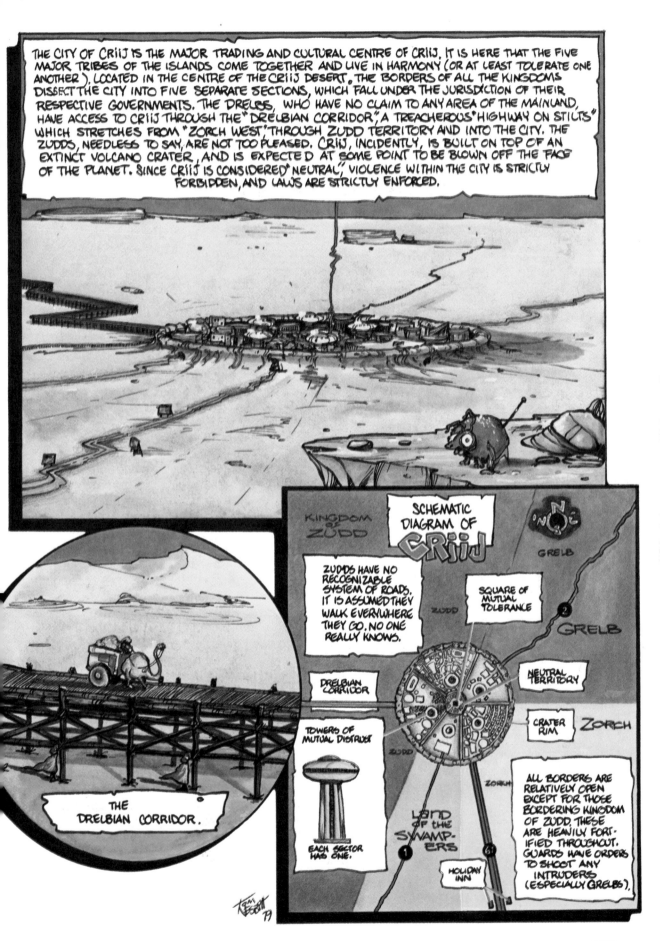

THE DRELBIAN CORRIDOR.

SCHEMATIC DIAGRAM OF CRIIJ

KINGDOM OF ZUDD

GRELB

ZUDDS HAVE NO RECOGNIZABLE SYSTEM OF ROADS. IT IS ASSUMED THEY WALK EVERYWHERE THEY GO. NO ONE REALLY KNOWS.

SQUARE OF MUTUAL TOLERANCE

ZUDD

GRELB

DRELBIAN CORRIDOR

NEUTRAL TERRITORY

CRATER RIM

ZORCH

TOWERS OF MUTUAL DISTRUST

ZUDD

EACH SECTOR HAS ONE.

ZORCH

LAND OF THE SWAMP-ERS

ALL BORDERS ARE RELATIVELY OPEN EXCEPT FOR THOSE BORDERING KINGDOM OF ZUDD. THESE ARE HEAVILY FORTIFIED THROUGHOUT. GUARDS HAVE ORDERS TO SHOOT ANY INTRUDERS (ESPECIALLY GRELBS).

HOLIDAY INN

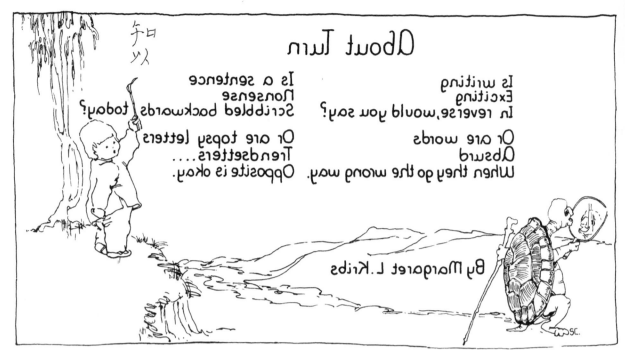

Forwards and Backwards

by: Margaret L. Kribs   *illustrations: Susan Cook*

Grab a pencil and write your name below using your right hand, then your left hand.

Right hand _____

Left hand _____

Do both of your signatures look the same? Or is one just a weird scrawl because you are normally right-handed and it was hard to write with your left hand. Or perhaps you are left-handed. Did you find it just as hard to sign your name with your right hand? Some left-handed people make more use of both hands. So, as a left-hander, you may be slightly better at writing with either hand. Why not check this out with a right-handed friend.

When you signed your name above, you wrote it, of course, from left to right. Now try writing your name (with either hand) in the opposite direction, from right to left.

_____ My name is

Your signature naturally looks backwards because we are accustomed to writing from left to right. At school, when you write in your exercise book, you are taught to start every line on the left side of the page. Yet there are some languages — Hebrew and Arabic, for example — which are written from right to left.

If you were writing Chinese, you would start at the top right-hand corner of the page. But instead of writing horizontally, you would place the characters (or words) one underneath the other in a column. Subsequent columns would go leftwards across the page.

At one time people even wrote forwards and backwards! Centuries ago the early Greeks and Romans alternated the direction of each line of their writing. They also reversed the letters on the left-to-right lines so that, in English, it would look like this:

First line is written from left to right
Next line is written from right to left
Again, this line goes from left to right
And this line reverses back to the left

This style of writing (not in use after the fifth century B.C.) was called *boustrophedon*, a Greek word meaning "ox-turning." You can see why when you picture an ox crossing a field as it ploughs a furrow, then turning, ready to plough the next furrow. You probably do the same sort of thing with the lawn mower when cutting the grass.

Can you imagine what it would be like to read a book with every other line printed backwards? A mirror might come in handy.

Certainly you would need a mirror to read the *Notebooks* of the famous fifteenth-century Italian painter, scientist and inventor, Leonardo da Vinci. He wrote all his notes in "mirror-writing"; all the letters and words of *every* line (not just alternate lines as in the *boustrophedon* style) are correctly formed in reverse and go from right to left.

Leonardo is supposed to have written his mirror-script notes with his left hand. Apparently people who write in mirror-script (He was not the only one!) usually do so with their left hand and without any previous practice.

Another famous person thought to have been left-handed is Lewis Carroll, author of *Alice's Adventures in Wonderland* and *Through the Looking-Glass*. He, too, could write backwards. To amuse his young friends, Carroll would write letters to them in mirror-script. Naturally he called this his "Looking-Glass writing." You may remember reading about Alice, as she sat watching the White King, finding a book which she thought was in some strange language. She puzzled over it until she realized it was a "Looking-glass book" and if she held it up to a mirror, the words would "all go the right way again."

127

Are You A Sinistral?

by: Barbara Wilson   illustrations: Mike Cherkas

in English, "awkward," "clumsy"; even "left" itself comes from the Old English word *lyft,* meaning "weak" or "worthless."

Since left-handers have to function in a right-hand oriented world, is it any wonder they occasionally appear awkward? How many right-handers could deftly open a can with an opener designed for left-handers? Isn't it possible they would seem "awkward" or "weak" in such a situation?

However, there is a compensation for left-handers; they often excel at sports. Since right-handers are usually faced with right-handed opponents, when they encounter a sinistral they're often thrown off guard, and have to learn a whole new set of tactics. Left-handers, "on the other hand," have had to learn unnatural methods from early childhood. Until recently, parents and

Perhaps you're a *sinistral* without even realizing it! If you're among the ten per cent or so of the population that is left-handed, then you *are* a sinistral.

The word comes from the Latin sinister meaning "left." When the Romans wanted to find clues in nature to explain or foretell happenings, they looked on signs from the right-hand side (e.g. a flock of birds flying past) as being "good" omens; those appearing on the left were of "evil" — or *sinister* — origin. Hence, the most common usage of the word *sinister* in our language today is "evil," or "menacing."

Nowadays we often hear of discrimination against minorities and the need for liberation. Well, what about the "rights" of left-handers? Historically, they've had a bad deal. In addition to being labelled with a word which is hardly flattering, sinistrals are described in other insulting terms: *gauche* (French for "left") means, teachers of left-handed children often forced them to use their right hands instead, sometimes with unhappy results.

Left-handedness has aroused curiosity over the centuries. Recently it has attracted serious scientific study. Just what causes sinistrality? Well, even after intensive research, the answer remains unclear. There are those who consider it an inherited characteristic — but how to prove this? True, statistically there are more left-handed children in families where both parents are left-handers. But this could equally be an argument for the influence of environment rather than heredity; the children may simply be copying their parents.

Other theories are many and varied. They range from the view that primitive man favoured right-hand usage to ensure a good aim at his enemy's heart with his sword or spear (the left hand functioning in a more passive role, holding a shield to guard his own heart), to the opinion held by an American doctor that left-handedness is caused by "emotional contrariness." He claims that out of a wish to oppose their parents' control, certain children try *not* to learn to be *dextral,* or right-handed!

It has been suggested that left-handedness may be caused by damage, at birth, to the left side of the brain (which controls functions on the right side of the body). This might

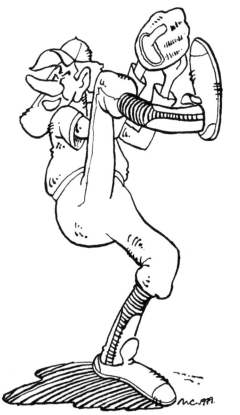

lead to the dominance of sinistral *laterality,* or "sidedness."

Whatever claim is made about left-handedness, an opposite proposition can be put forward. Even studies done to show the extent of left-handedness vary in their results between 1 and 36%, though a generally held figure is around 10%. Other studies, which indicate that such groups as criminals and neurotics have high proportions of left-handers in their numbers, are countered by evidence that left-handers also figure disproportionately as outstandingly successful individuals — even geniuses!

If you are left-handed, you can take comfort that you are in good company. Perhaps because they have had to struggle so hard in a right-handed world, sinistrals have a significant number of outstanding individuals in their ranks. Joan of Arc, Julius Caesar, Leonardo da Vinci, Napoleon Bonaparte, Albert Einstein, Marilyn Monroe and Paul McCartney have all exerted a great influence on society.

Apparently we're still a long way from solving the mysteries of left-handedness. Meanwhile sinistrals can band together to form their own "liberation groups"; this is happening already in large centres like New York, London, and Toronto. They can even get on mailing lists for catalogues of gadgets designed for left-handers, and find other materials of interest only to themselves.

As my left-handed daughter claims, "Sinistrals have a 'right' to be left." I'm a dextral myself, but I agree with her. I'd only add, "But they don't have a right to be 'left' alone with their problems." So if you're a dextral, the next time you see a "leftie" having difficulties in this right-handed world, put yourself in his (or her) position; it's more difficult than you think!

Some tests to find if you're a *sinistral:*

1 Clap your hands — which hand is uppermost?
2 Draw a circle — if you draw it in a *clockwise* direction, chances are you're a sinistral.
3 Scratch the centre of your back — which hand did you use?
4 Tilt your head sideways towards one shoulder — which shoulder did it touch?
5 Fold your arms — which forearm is uppermost?

You'll probably find that you're neither wholly sinistral nor dextral; most people aren't. But one side usually takes the dominant role, or "upper hand."

Dawson, Yukon Territories, circa 1899.

Canadiana Quiz

by: Rosemary Lunardini   *photos: Public Archives of Canada*

Early settlers in all parts of Canada often wrote diaries and letters which described the awakening land they had found. Women pioneers were especially good writers, keeping journals of their travels and recording events in their diaries when the day was done. Some of them became famous, but most remain unknown — except for the written records they left. Their letters are kept in libraries, the broken sealing wax still clinging to them. Their diaries bear a fancy, quaint hand-writing on the yellowed pages of tiny notebooks.

Here are excerpts from the writings of ten women. Each of them describes a *place* in the country settled or visited. It could be a province, a town, a river, or even a building. See how many places you can name!

1. *In the very earliest days of settlement, friendship was established . . . by the French-Canadians and the Métis who showed warmhearted kindness to the poor Scottish people when the lack of food at the Forks compelled them to go down to the buffalo hunters' headquarters at the mouth of the Pembina River in the winter time.*

2. *We drove on the ice to Skinner's Mill, a mile beyond Castle Frank, which looked beautiful from the river. At the mouth of the Don I fished from my cariole, but the fish are not to be caught as they were last winter, several dozen in an hour. It is said the*

noise . . . driving constantly over this ice frightens away the fish, which seems probable, for they are still in abundance in the Humber, where we do not drive.

3. *With plenty of money or gold dust it was sometimes difficult to get enough to eat, as the storekeepers had to deal out provisions sparingly to guard against a shortage before the new supplies arrived in the spring.*

4. *Rafts of squared timber and of rough logs running up to hundreds of lock bands, built up with cook and bunk houses, stables for horses . . . made their slow way to mills and market every year . . . I have seen the men at work without a break for over sixty hours. They slept on the grass while the locks were*

Winter fishing, Assynoibain and Red River, 1821.

Curling on Don River, Toronto.

Bonsecours Church, Montreal, founded 1657.

filling and ate their meals that had been brought to them sitting on a swing bar. They worked 24 hours a day and slept when they could. At first the lock men were paid sixty cents a day for seven and a half months each year. Later their pay was raised to one dollar a day and there was never a time when there was any trouble in getting men to work on the locks. And now it is done.

5. The Picture Gallery is the only room fit to visit and it was there we had luncheon. We saw the model of the Library which will be a most splendid building. It is made of Plaster of Paris and kept in a room to show what the Library will be. We went quite up to the top and saw such a nice view . . . The Chaudiere Falls are very pretty and can be seen very well from there.

6. It was a beautiful day, clear and bright, but when they were returning home, they noticed a darkening of the sky, but no clouds were visible . . . Just then there was another darkening of the sky, and down fell such a strange shower, the like of which they had never beheld before. Soon everything was covered with (a) green, hopping, wriggling mess. "Grasshoppers," exclaimed Mrs. Graham. "Now the country is ruined; for they will eat all the crops." Sure enough, they made great havoc of them and there was little reaped that season.

7. Got up in the morning and found ourselves nigh to land on both sides . . . Our ship anchored off against Fort Howe in Saint John's River. Our people went on shore and brought on board pea vines with blossoms on them, gooseberries, spruce and grass . . . It is, I think, the roughest land I ever saw. We are all ordered to land tomorrow and not a shelter to go under.

8. The country along the shores of the Lake very barren, and rugged, the fantastic shapes of the rocks forming the chief variety:

"North" Canoe on Lake Superior, 1857.

two of these situated in the Lake a little distance from the shore, of a considerable height, and almost perpendicular, were formerly worshiped by the Indians, who used to sacrifice human victims to appease the wrath of the Evil Spirit whom they supposed to inhabit them.

9. The town . . . is large, and the spires of the churches, covered with tin, give a brilliance to the scene and look like mosques. The country around is much cultivated, and orchards cover nearly all the top of the mountain.

10. All the world goes past my door — I see land seekers going north, and further north . . . It's rather thrilling to see them; the men and their wives and families; their stoves, pots and pans, bedsteads, and sometimes children's toys and violins and weird oddments on the wagon; an odd cow and dog or two running behind; the whole procession moving at about three miles an hour. There's something astounding about their courage when they arrive, miles from anywhere.

ANSWERS TO CANADIANA QUIZ

1. The Red River settlement. Janet Bannerman, born in 1840, was the child of Red River settlers and recalled her life there in the book Women of Red River.

Houses of Parliament, Ottawa, circa 1870.

Partridge Island and the harbour, Saint John, N.B., 1835.

Settler's Cabin, Alberta, 1921.

2. York (Toronto). From the journal of Mrs. John Graves Simcoe, wife of the Lieutenant Governor of Upper Canada, February, 1796. Castle Frank was built for her young son, Francis.

3. Dawson City, Yukon, in the days of the Klondike Gold Rush. Ella Hall was a young woman from Boston who went to the Yukon in 1898 to seek her fortune.

4. The Rideau Canal. This unidentified writer in the Tweedsmuir Books lived near Jones Falls in the mid-1800's.

5. Parliament Buildings in Ottawa. Mercy Ann Coles must have been one of the first people to tour Parliament, for the building was not yet finished when she visited in 1864. She lived in Prince Edward Island.

6. "The Prairies" is good enough! It was near Portage la Prairie, Manitoba, that Mary Morrison Brown homesteaded with her parents in 1874 when she was twelve years old.

7. Saint John, New Brunswick, formerly called Parr Town, Nova Scotia. From the diary of Sarah Frost, June 28, 1784. Sarah was one of thousands of Loyalists who sailed from New York after the American Revolution. Many on her ship were sick with measles. A few weeks after landing at Saint John, Sarah's daughter was born.

8. Lake Superior. Frances Simpson was the eighteen-year-old bride of George Simpson of the Hudson's Bay Company. She is well-known for a journal of her trip and drawings of her journey by canoe with the Voyageurs from Montreal to Red River and to Hudson Bay in 1830.

9. Montreal. From the diary of Mrs. Simcoe, June, 1792.

10. Alberta. Mary Percy Jackson was a pioneer doctor for the 350-square-mile district of Battle River, Alberta. From letters she wrote home to England in 1929, published in The Beaver.

Tutankhamun's Tomb Discovered

by: Mary E. Culbert   *photos: Art Gallery of Ontario*

Archaeologist Howard Carter learned the hard way that patience is indeed a virtue. He searched diligently for six successive seasons — October to April — under hot Egyptian skies before finally discovering the tomb of Tutankhamun.

From 1914 to 1922, in partnership with Lord Carnarvon, Howard Carter focused all his vast archaeological training upon one decisive moment — "the moment of truth," as he expressed it. Would he find the boy-king's tomb on the small site in the rocky Valley of the Kings? Carter felt strongly that there were still tombs awaiting discovery there. He admits in his writings that he "almost dared to hope" that this was so.

Burial grounds for the pharaohs of the New Kingdom era (1590-1085 B.C.) were difficult to reach, built purposely to discourage plundering by tomb robbers. They consisted of one or more corridors and a series of rooms, some extending hundreds of feet into the rock.

Before Carter joined Lord Carnarvon he worked for another excavator, who had found a cache of large jars of baked clay with seal impressions bearing the name of Tutankhamun. The jars contained the discarded materials and equipment that had been used during the funeral ceremonies of the young king. While most scholars were certain that this was all that remained of the ruler's tomb, Carter believed that the pharaoh was buried in the vicinity — and that with persistence, his search would end successfully.

Until the 1900's few facts were known of Tutankhamun's tomb or his reign. Mention was hardly made of it by guides who led swarms of tourists through the Valley of the Kings. The boy-pharaoh had ruled for only nine years, coming to the throne about 1371 B.C. as a lad of eleven. He was married to either a niece or a sister. His name originally had been Tutankhaten, in honour of the god Aten (the sun-disc), whom he worshipped. Gradually he was weaned from his childhood devotion to the Aten and his name was changed to Tutankhamun, after Amun, chief god of Thebes. A number of objects found in the tomb have associations with Aten; these are associated with Tutankhamun's life prior to his name change.

Politics — as well as religion — was in a state of confusion and corruption during the reign of Tutankhamun. The young, passionate monarch neglected his duties as military commander and head of government, and his Egyptian empire started to crumble. Could he have been murdered by some ruthless politician? Who knows?

Driven by intense curiosity, but using logic — and patience — Howard Carter made a large-scale map of the Valley floor. He subdivided it into sections to make sure that every square inch would be examined thoroughly. Because Lord Carnarvon wanted to return home to England, Carter was left in 1917 to work on his own. He discovered nothing that year, nor in 1918.

The years passed. During the

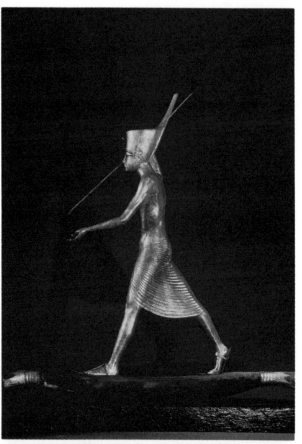

summer of 1922 Carnarvon summoned Carter to England to discuss their partnership. After the First World War (1914-1918) ended, money was scarce and Carnarvon threatened to withdraw his financial support. Carter begged for one more season at the digs. His map showed a small triangular area, just below the tomb of Rameses VI, not checked out. Carnarvon, still a sportsman and a gambler, promised to finance one more season.

The optimistic Carter returned to Luxor, Egypt, on October 28, 1922. On November 1st he and his workmen started digging in the area below the tomb of Rameses.

On November 4th, silent workmen awaited Carter. What was their problem? They had discovered a step cut into the rock under a workmen's hut, only two yards away from the point where a previous excavator had left off.

Carter could clearly see the entrance to a tomb. He tried to remain calm. It might have been abandoned, or plundered and stripped of everything valuable long ago. Carter knew that every royal tomb found so far had been looted within a few years of burial.

The stairway down into the rocky hillside was completely filled with rubble. At the bottom he found a blocked doorway, plastered and sealed with the name of Tutankhamun. The seals were unbroken! Carter made a small hole in the top of the door and saw another passage, also completely filled with rubble.

"I needed all my self-control to keep from breaking down the doorway, and investigating then and there," Carter wrote. "It was a thrilling moment for an excavator."

But Carter had an obligation to Lord Carnarvon, his partner, and wanted him on the site to share the special "moment of truth." Carter refilled the stairway and posted a guard. Next morning, November 7th, he sent this historic telegram to his patron:

At last you have made wonderful discovery in Valley. A magnificent tomb with seals intact. Re-covered same for your arrival. Congratulations. Carter.

Lord Carnarvon arrived in Egypt on November 23rd with his daughter, Lady Evelyn Herbert, and work was restarted. The doorway was broken down and the corridor behind it cleared of stone chippings. All artifacts were painstakingly recorded. On November 28th, thirty feet down from the entrance, they discovered a second doorway sealed with impressions of the name Tutankhamun.

Carter's hands trembled as he made a tiny opening in the upper left-hand corner of the doorway and probed inside with a testing rod. He described his first glimpse through a widened hole into the Antechamber: "At first I could see nothing, the hot air escaping from the chamber causing the candle flame to flicker, but presently, as my eyes grew accustomed to the light, details of the room within emerged slowly from the mist,

strange animals, statues and gold — everywhere the glint of gold."

Lord Carnarvon, beside himself with suspense, questioned Carter anxiously, "Can you see anything?"

"Yes, wonderful things."

The view before Carter was incredible, like a scene from a glorious fairy tale. The ancient Egyptians, believing that life after death must resemble life before, buried an individual's belongings — including weapons, games, clothing and food — with the body. Tutankhamun had obviously been a very rich king indeed. The four-chambered tomb was filled with furniture, never surpassed in the perfection of its workmanship and decoration, fine linen and exquisitely carved alabaster vases such as the world has never seen, and gold! Gold everywhere! In the words of Professor James Breasted, an American Egyptologist, " . . . all the heaped-up riches of a king who had died some 3,250 years ago."

The Burial Chamber (21' x 13') was all but filled by an immense gold shrine, beautifully decorated in relief with blue faience (earthenware decorated with opaque, colourful glazes). Inside this was another gold shrine, draped with a linen pall, with precious objects between the two. Two more gold shrines inside this protected the magnificent stone sarcophagus.

It took seventy days for the ancient Egyptians to mummify a body, and this was considered the official period of mourning. If the ruler had been long-lived, a sepulchre would have been prepared during his lifetime. This insignificant boy-king must have had his tomb dug rather hastily. It was a very humble and inconspicuous affair compared to the vast tombs of the great pharaohs who preceded him. But Carter's accident of archaeology made Tutankhamun the most celebrated Egyptian ruler, with the possible exception of Cleopatra.

When the stone lide of the sarcophagus was raised, the fine linen shrouds were carefully rolled back, one by one. Carter records, " . . . a gasp of wonderment escaped our lips, so gorgeous was the sight that met our eyes; a gold effigy of the young boy-king, of most magnificent workmanship, filled the whole sarcophagus."

The mummy lay in the third and final coffin, decorated lavishly with beaten gold and inlaid jewels. His head was covered with the well-known gold death mask, now one of the world's most famous art treasures. With scrupulous care and patience, using a soft sable brush, the last few fragments of fabric fell away, revealing a remarkably refined and cultured countenance.

Howard Carter spent the next ten seasons clearing the splendid treasures from Tutankhamun's four-chambered tomb, and moving them to the National Museum in Cairo.

The workers had to move slowly to avoid damaging this fantastic cache, and to carefully record every item. A long task — yet the young ruler's tomb and contents were extremely modest compared to the elaborate burial places of other rulers, such as Rameses II. Left behind, and still resting in its outer coffin in the tomb, was the mummified body of Tutankhamun himself.

Because dedicated people persisted for years in their search for the tombs of the pharaohs, painstakingly recording and preserving what was found, precious treasures have been saved from further damage or plundering. And we have learned how once-nomadic tribesmen developed the social and economic patterns that brought them out of the Stone Age into a modern civilization.

*Canopic Jars

May You Live For Millions Of Years

(WARNING: This article is not for the squeamish!)

by: Arthur R. Jamieson, Education Services, Royal Ontario Museum
photos: Brian Boyle and Bill Robertson (Royal Ontario Museum)

Mummies! The word itself creates nervous excitement; our imaginations dance with thoughts of frightening horror movies; stories of curses and death to those who discover a mummy's tomb, tales of treasures, and others — not always true — of a great and mighty civilization.

Religion had an enormous impact on the life of the ancient Egyptians, and was very influential in their civilization. Great concern was shown towards their dead and the afterlife. For its continued existence in the next world, the body had to be preserved. If the corpse was destroyed, the person — or animal — could not enjoy a life in heaven with the gods, for the soul would be condemned to search forever in vain for a body which no longer existed. The ancient Egyptian would have been horrified to think that Canadians sometimes use fire — cremation — to dispose of their dead.

To ensure the survival of the body after death, the ancient Egyptians practised mummification. This process was very expensive, and not everyone could afford it. Those who could had several "grades" to choose from, and the family would select the one which fit into their budget — much as is done today when picking a funeral for a family member.

The priests and embalmers usually took great care that the body was properly mummified. After death it was taken to the embalmers, who would work their art on the deceased. Throughout the process of mummification, priests recited prayers and funerary texts appropriate to each step in the procedure.

First, anything within the body which might cause decay was removed. The brain was extracted through the nostrils with a metal hook, and usually discarded. Then the head was flushed with cheap wine or drugs to dissolve any remaining matter. Next, an incision was made on the lower left side of the torso, using an

Mummy of a cat which shows elaborate wrapping. Royal Ontario Museum.

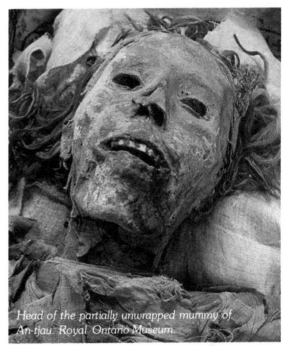

Head of the partially unwrapped mummy of An-tjau. Royal Ontario Museum.

Mummy of a hawk in its faience coffin. Royal Ontario Museum.

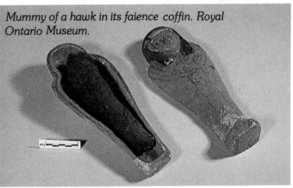

"Ethiopian cutting stone" (perhaps obsidian), and four major organs of the chest cavity were removed and dried out. The four organs (the viscera) were usually placed in containers called Canopic jars, which were later buried with the body. The chest cavity was then stuffed with a dry chemical called *natron* and the outside of the body packed in natron and salt. The body was left in the chemicals for as long as forty days to remove the water. The internal organs were dried in the same manner. About 75% of the body is water, but after the drying process little was left except skin and bones.

The body was then washed, and sometimes dried in the hot sun. Perfumes, oils, spices, cloth, and occasionally mud were put into the abdomen. The outside of the body was anointed with oils and perfumes to soften the skin and help preserve it. It was then carefully wrapped with linen.

The linen strips wrapped around the body were of considerable length; the best prepared mummies were wrapped in several hundred yards of bandages. The fingers, hands, and feet were wrapped separately, and padding was sometimes used around the body while it was being wrapped entirely with larger linen strips. Sometimes the bandages were soaked in an adhesive material to make them stick together. Amulets were placed in the bandages, as these charms were thought to help preserve and protect the deceased. Sometimes mummy masks were placed over the head and shoulders of a wrapped body. Now the individual was ready for its coffin and funeral service.

The pharaoh Tutankhamun ("King Tut") was embalmed like this, but the oils in the ungents and ointments used on his body proved to be too strong and much of the skin has disappeared. The embalmers obviously had not been careful enough in their work!

Many exciting stories exist about the "mummy's curse" placed on the body and tomb of Tutankhamun, but they are all untrue. The original story of the curse was dreamed up by a newspaper reporter for his readers! People generally love mystery and horror stories, and the fictional stories which abound concerning curses are exciting and make intriguing reading.

The ancient Egyptians believed that if you mentioned a dead person's name, you would help him to live forever. The great wish was, "May you live for millions of years!" At the end of the mummification process, these words were recited: "You will live again, you will live again forever! Behold, you are young again forever!"

*Canopic Jars. The liver was placed in the jar with the human-headed top representing the god Imseti. The lungs were put in the jar with the baboon-headed top representing the god Hapy. The jackel-headed jar representing the god Duamutef held the stomach. The falcon-headed jar representing the god Qebehsenuf held the intestines. Royal Ontario Museum.

~ RANGER BOB'S ~
NATURE NOTE-PAD

WHY IS IT THAT WHEN A KANGAROO HOPS AS FAST AS 65 KILOMETERS (44 MILES) PER HOUR, IT IS NEVER WINDED?

THE ANSWER LIES IN THE EXTRA-ORDINARY STORAGE CAPACITY OF ITS *ACHILLES TENDON* — THE TENDON THAT JOINS THE CALF TO THE HEEL. WHEN THE KANGAROO HOPS FAST, THE TENDON ACTS AS A SPRING.

WHEN THE KANGAROO INCREASES ITS SPEED, IT ALSO INCREASES ITS FORCE AND STORES MORE ENERGY IN THE *ACHILLES TENDONS*, THEREFORE MEANING THAT THE AMOUNT OF ENERGY STORED IS PROPORTIONAL TO THE FORCE ACTING ON IT.

~ ©79 • POLIWKO • THEOBALDS ~

Puzzles by Bill Ettridge   Illustrations by Arn Saba with David Roman

The Cross Crossword Puzzle

Clues Across.

3. Identification (Abr.)
5. Myself
6. Meadow
8. Tear
9. Cooking fat
11. Throw
12. Peruse with eyes
14. Vases
15. Land measure
17. Tie
18. Listeners
20. Speech impediment
21. Sickness
23. Like an exam (3 words)
24. Slender shaft
25. Collections
27. Grows from scalp
28. To reduce speed
30. Mineral powder
31. Nobleman
33. Dumb
34. Recompensed
36. Exist (Plural)
37. Normal value (Golf)
38. Not out
39. Royal Academy (Abr.)

Clues Down.

1. Beak
2. Maintained
4. Expensive
5. Young lady
7. Length times width
8. Preach noisily
10. Fish
11. Riding whip
13. Theatrical
14. Disturb
16. Obliterator
17. Busses with lips
19. Close door violently
20. Untruths
22. -- home, not away
24. Transaction for cash
26. Cleanser
27. Dislike greatly
29. Envelop as a parcel
30. Change direction
32. Teller of untruths
33. Household servant
35. Trail behind

Diamond Maze

143

ABC Diamond Word Puzzle

Starting with the single letter "A", solve the clues by adding or subtracting one letter only and rearranging the letters of the preceding answer.

A

Clue	Answer
Royal Artillery	_ _
Listener	_ _ _
Garden tool	_ _ _ _
Snap or smash	_ _ _ _ _
Drinking glass	_ _ _ _ _ _
Car stopper	_ _ _ _ _
Unclothed	_ _ _ _
Saloon	_ _ _
Ordinary seaman	_ _

B

Clue	Answer
Arts graduate	_ _
Hired public transport	_ _ _
Clawed sea food	_ _ _ _
Two or strut	_ _ _ _ _
Break, as a promise	_ _ _ _ _ _
Stretch out for	_ _ _ _ _
Bridge support	_ _ _ _
Vehicle	_ _ _
Alternating current	_ _

C

Clue	Answer
Direct current	_ _
Mean fellow	_ _ _
Covered with or·in	_ _ _ _
Tied up, as a shoe	_ _ _ _ _
Wax stick	_ _ _ _ _ _
Waltz or polka	_ _ _ _ _
Resident of Denmark	_ _ _ _ _
Also	_ _ _
District Attorney	_ _

D

Ye Durance Vile

HEY!

DON'T WORRY ABOUT A T'ING, FOLKS! JAILS HAS BACK DOORS, TOO!

NEVAIR 'AVE I BEEN SO HUMIDIFIED!

NICE DAY! YES? NO? UNCOMMITTED?

His, Her, and Our Words

The six words shown by dashes below each contain the word HIS. Can you solve the clues?

_ _ _ _ _ _	A card game
_ _ _ _ _ _ _	A cutting tool
_ _ _ _ _ _ _ _	A prickly plant
_ _ _ _ _ _ _	Now past
_ _ _ _ _ _ _	Sounds of displeasure
_ _ _ _ _ _ _	Shrill sound

Now we have six HER words. What are they?

_ _ _ _ _ _	Long legged bird
_ _ _ _ _ _ _	A globe
_ _ _ _ _ _ _ _	A cigar
_ _ _ _ _ _ _ _	Rising current of warm air
_ _ _ _ _ _ _	A fruit
_ _ _ _ _ _	Sleeping gas

Lastly we have OUR words.

_ _ _ _ _	A number
_ _ _ _ _ _	Ground meal
_ _ _ _ _ _	Diversion
_ _ _ _ _ _ _	Bravery
_ _ _ _ _ _	Be sorrowful
_ _ _ _ _	Grim

LARGE WEATHER WE'RE HAVING !

A New Year Cryptic Puzzle

If you are tired of crossword puzzles having one-word clues, or would like to tackle more involved brain teasers, welcome to the world of the CRYPTIC CROSSWORD. The word "cryptic" means "secret" or "hidden", so be prepared for some hard thinking! The following examples of clues and answers show how to solve the puzzle.

Clue. *Revise team for food.* Answer. MEAT
ANAGRAM — An anagram is a word formed by rearranging the letters of another word. In this example TEAM is rearranged to read MEAT.

Clue. *Find danger in paper illness.* Answer. PERIL
BURIED WORD — Here the answer is hidden — paper illness.

Clue. *Time sounds like yours and mine.* Answer. HOURS
SOUND WORDS — Quite simply, yours and mine = ours, which sounds like HOURS, and hours measure time.

Clue. *A hot singer.* Answer. KETTLE
DOUBLE MEANING — Kettles are said to "sing" as the water turns to steam.

Now, brush up your brains, point up your pencil, and tackle A NEW YEAR CRYPTIC PUZZLE.

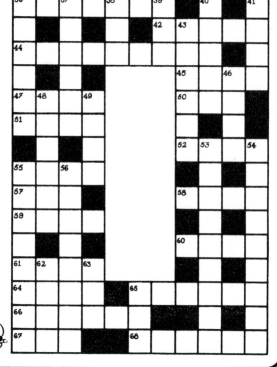

Clues across.

1. Spin wee yarn for the 1st.
7. Robes easily hides one who is this.
9. Controller with a great rule?
10. Guns, close to hands?
12. Race around a land measure.
15. Bread in starry eyes.
16. Leaning ship on the table?
17. Lost rice in a monk's walk.
22. Does he build bow bridges?
24. Dog hides in curried rice.
25. Gray men of divided country.
26. Continent of Siamese cats.
27. There's one where there's a way they say.
28. Where Ringo hides Ireland.
31. I'm in about for small size.
32. Cast in or about highjinks.
33. Fit Alice hides sloping type.
34. Short state in scale.
35. Tea with moan sounding string.

Clues down.

1. It's usual to switch Roman L.
2. Sew rag and produce bets.
3. A fish hides in feeling.
4. Carrot without vehicle decays.
5. Fruit in October rye bread.
6. Find writers in open school.
8. So drab makes stage lumber.
11. Old lake found in some repair.
13. Sir cur is found in high cloud.
14. Engrave on a wet Christian.
18. Gel for one to stand on.
19. Is roe a metal fish?
20. Dint ratio as a custom.
21. Rail toys for a monarchist.
22. Cad I came to be scholarly.
23. Lawbreaker nixes in marlic.
29. For I take a hidden girl.
30. Lin, is she a girl for nought?
32. Pretend it's a government bill.

> This is the halfway point. If you wish, take a look at the answer now, but be sure to cover the second part! Can you see how the clues are solved? Right, now try the second part — I hope you get zero, if you see what I mean.

Clues across.

36. Roc to be a month.
42. Scouter lacks science without.
44. Children's Christmas show.
45. Gone, sounds as if it was overtaken.
47. This bodied seaman can do?
50. Dig in simply for devil.
51. Want to change eden.
52. Ache for individual ones.
55. With a ruse be certain.
57. The supper hour I hear.
58. Puck frozen from end to end?
59. Kind of printing, sound.
60. Girlish money in India?
61. Cut a pear to harvest.
64. Dean from Denmark.
65. Brass killer hides one talent.
66. Heavens in fast rally car.
67. The affirmative in red eyes.
68. Sounds as if shovel's partner and cut join for outdoor meal.

Clues down.

36. Harp on for no parents.
37. Smart in patting legs.
38. If timid, wouldn't say it to a goose.
39. Endless broil a French king.
40. All mates turn to vapour.
41. Jog with tea before decay.
43. Trump Ireland has a referee.
46. Span's friend, also tidy.
48. Yea but is lovely if stirred.
49. The rim of hedges.
53. An Easter uprising.
54. Rich lady U change water system.
55. Do we not stand on this day?
56. Strap Len and seed again.
62. Relax in released state.
63. Persia starts Latin through.
65. Can a pal change a mountain?

THE BEST DEFENSE IS TA BE TOTALLY OFFENSIVE!

148

The Big One

Two sets of clues are offered with which to solve this puzzle —
You may use either one or both sets to find the answer.

SIMPLE CLUES.

Across.

1. From now on.
5. White notes.
8. Roof covering.
10. Attics.
11. Great! (slang)
13. Short holiday.
14. Poems.
15. Afternoon meals.
18. Beneath.
20. Has 24 hours.
21. Before. (poetic)
23. Lightly cooked.
25. Long river.
29. A devil.
30. Let drop.

Down.

1. Long period.
2. Consume.
3. Market.
4. Revolve along.
6. Landing ground.
7. Numb.
9. Conflict.
12. Of a tree.
15. Piano adjuster.
16. One who sums.
17. Ocean.
19. Grain.
22. Allowance. (food)
24. Painting stand.
25. Insane.
26. Total.
27. Orange seed.
28. Rage.

CRYPTIC CLUES.

Across.

1. Remove 'er for always.
5. Salt a run for white keys.
8. Stiles hides a shingle.
10. Attics start fan in lots.
11. Seas well show wave motion.
13. Short vac'n leads holly.
14. Verses, does do switch.
15. Move a seat for drinks.
18. Below in ground error.
20. Night's partner has Danny losing poles.
21. There ends before.
23. Rear twist is uncommon.
25. River from sip, I miss sip.
29. Me and Lon confuse a devil.
30. Memory slip sounds like track circuits.

Down.

1. Long time in the onset.
2. Consume in seating plan.
3. Tram returns to market.
4. Brolly has a turn over.
6. Vapour meadow for planes?
7. No taste, or brains perhaps.
9. Cymbal sound of music lashing.
12. Tree fibre shakes O.E. down.
15. Harmonizer from Trune.
16. Snake has mathematical idea.
17. Waterbody has a look I hear.
19. Fair yellow field has a grain crop.
22. Assigned portion, in a rot.
24. Please look hides a canvas support.
25. Madeline starts wildly foolish.
26. Assume, it has a total.
27. Little dog runs backwards and forwards.
28. Myself and short reference join in anger.

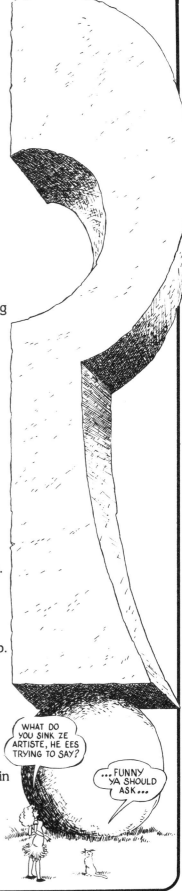

Clueless Crosswords

Crossword puzzles without clues!
The answers are given to you. Just put them into the
correct places to complete the puzzles.
One simple hint — compare the numbers of letters in the answers,
and the number of boxes available in the crossword.

NUMBER 1

Across.
Ant
Sir
Amen
Cone
Peat
Shim
Adore
Dairy
Parent
Totems

Down.
Hoe
Met
Tap
Tea
Area
Isis
Topo
Your
Drome
Inner
Ardent
Scream

NUMBER 2

Across.
Ago
Ass
Imp
Rag
Heap
Nine
Moral
Sit in
Manitoba
Winnipeg

Down.
Ewer
Exam
Neon
Pray
Isolip
No snag
Pairing
Station

Hidden Homophones

A homophone is one of two or more words which sound alike but have different meanings. First solve the clues for the two columns, and then match the like sounding words. To make it easier for you, all the words in the left column start with the letter "A", and all the words in the right column are nouns (things). Two examples are given to start you off.

#	Clue (left)	Answer	#	Clue (right)	Answer
1.	Out of order	A M I S S	1.	A leap	A _ _ _ _ _ _
2.	Oak fruit	A _ _ _ _ _	2.	A lamp	A _ _ _ _ _ _
3.	In front of	A _ _ _ _ _	3.	Above neck	A _ _ _ _ _
4.	Alongside	A _ _ _ _ _	4.	Single lady	A M I S S
5.	Upward	A _ _ _ _ _ _	5.	A poem	A _ _ _ _ _ _
6.	Plentiful	A _ _ _ _ _ _	6.	A ray	A _ _ _ _
7.	Side to side	A _ _ _ _ _ _	7.	A piece	A _ _ _ _
8.	Opposed	A _ _ _ _ _	8.	A grain	A _ _ _ _
9.	Separated	A _ _ _ _	9.	A smell	A _ _ _ _ _ _
10.	Dismount	A _ _ _ _ _ _	10.	Crucifix	A _ _ _ _ _ _
11.	Concerning	A _ _ _ _ _	11.	A dot	A _ _ _ _ _ _
12.	Event	A _ _ _ _ _ _	12.	A fight	A _ _ _ _
13.	Assign	A L L O T	13.	A closure	A _ _ _ _ _
14.	Put in office	A _ _ _ _ _ _ _ _	14.	Big number	A L O T
15.	Love deeply	A _ _ _ _ _	15.	Sideshow	A _ _ _ _ _
16.	Attack	A _ _ _ _ _ _	16.	A string	A _ _ _ _ _
17.	Challenge	A _ _ _ _ _ _	17.	Set of bells	A _ _ _ _ _
18.	Agreement	A _ _ _ _ _ _	18.	A pitch	A _ _ _ _ _
19.	Make up for	A _ _ _ _ _	19.	An expense	A _ _ _ _ _
20.	Attraction	A _ _ _ _ _ _	20.	Windmill arm	A _ _ _ _ _

Rebus Riddles

REBUS means a "picture word". Can you read the proverbs that follow?

A Rhyming Puzzle

Solve the clues, and then read the initial letters of the answers from top to bottom to spell out a seasonal activity of our feathered friends.

Here's a hint. The last syllables of the words in each group have the same sound, although not necessarily the same spelling. For example — debate, weight, great.

Thought centre.   _ _ _ _ _ _

Crazy.   _ _ _ _ _ _ _

Rule from a throne.   _ _ _ _ _ _

Draw off with a ditch.   _ _ _ _ _ _

Discolouring mark.   _ _ _ _ _ _

Honest and open.   _ _ _ _ _ _

Long and lifeless.   _ _ _ _ _

Tug or pull.   _ _ _ _

One of four in year.   _ _ _ _ _ _ _

Strong smelling vegetable.   _ _ _ _ _ _

Released from ties.   _ _ _ _ _ _ _

Sinew — muscle to bone.   _ _ _ _ _ _

Listen.   _ _ _ _ _ _

Brainwave.   _ _ _ _ _

Close by.   _ _ _ _

Crease in fabric.   _ _ _ _ _ _ _

Frozen water hanging.   _ _ _ _ _ _ _

Quick or fleet.   _ _ _ _ _ _

Finger protection.   _ _ _ _ _ _ _

Good behaviour.   _ _ _ _ _ _ _

Has extreme views.   _ _ _ _ _ _ _

Travelways

There are sixty-six words buried in this word game. Some are written backwards, some read from top to bottom, others from bottom to top, and some diagonally. See how many you can find. The first word — ACTION — is ringed as an example.

```
L  I  N  E  R  R  E  L  A  E  S  O  O  B  A  C
P  O  A  S  E  N  A  L  P  L  I  A  S  A  N  D
R  A  C  I  N  G  I  C  A  B  S  W  I  T  C  H
A  U  T  O  M  O  B  I  L  E  I  E  H  C  H  O
T  C  I  H  M  L  W  A  Y  I  R  C  D  O  O  W
N  A  O  S  L  O  O  P  A  L  A  A  Y  A  R  D
I  R  N  I  A  R  T  L  L  Y  R  R  W  C  N  B
A  A  I  D  S  B  I  I  A  O  I  T  O  H  L  R
W  V  S  P  E  A  R  W  V  P  U  K  C  I  P  E
A  A  U  I  R  M  F  E  R  E  U  G  S  H  P  D
H  N  O  T  A  O  R  A  T  R  L  S  H  I  R  I
S  Y  C  A  T  A  M  A  R  A  N  A  H  R  E  L
K  A  G  H  A  C  K  T  R  I  P  S  N  E  L  G
C  N  G  G  T  S  O  L  W  A  R  T  L  G  L  A
I  I  A  S  U  B  M  A  R  I  N  E  P  O  I  W
R  E  G  R  A  B  A  R  A  C  T  E  E  R  T  S
```

Action	Coach	Right-of-way	Spear
Airship	Cousin	Roger	Streetcar
Anchor		Rover	Submarine
Arab	Dhow		Swag
Area	Dray	Sabre	Switch
Asia		Sailplane	
Automobile	Gas	Sand	Tandem
	Glider	Safari	Tiller
Barge		Open	Scow	Train
Bicycle	Hack	Opal	Sealer	Trail
Bliss	Hire		Sedan	Trawl
Buggy		Path	Signal	Trips
	Liner	Pickup	Skate	Truck
Caboose	Locomotive		Ski	
Caravan	Lost	Racing	Sloop	Wain
Cart		Railcar	Slot	Yacht
Catamaran	Oil	Rank	Snowplough	Yawl
		Rickshaw		

HOW KIN ANYBODY BE BOTHERED?

CROSS CROSSWORD

Across: 3. i.d. 5. me 6. lea 8. rip 9. lard 11. cast 12. read 14. urns 15. acre 17. knot 18. ears 20. lisp 21. malaise 23. as a test 24. stem 25. sets 27. hair 28. slow 30. talc 31. earl 33. mute 34. pail 36. are 37. par 38. in 39. R.A.

Down: 1. bill 2. kept 4. dear 5. miss 7. area 8. rant 10. dace 11. crop 13. dramatic 14. unsettle 16. eraser 17. kisses 19. slam 20. lies 22. at 24. sale 26. soap 27. hate 29. wrap 30. turn 32. liar 33. maid 35. drag

THE BIG ONE

Across: 1. evermore 5. naturals 8. tile 10. lofts 11. swell 13. hol 14. odes 15. teas 18. under 20. day 21. ere 23. rare 25. Mississippi 29. demon 30. lapse

Down: 1. eon 2. eat 3. mart 4. roll 6. airfield 7. senseless 9. clash 12. wooden 15. tuner 16. adder 17. sea 19. rye 22. ration 24. easel 25. mad 26. sum 27. pip 28. ire

NEW YEAR CRYPTIC

Across: 1. New year 7. obese 9. regulator 10. arms 12. acre 15. rye 16. list 17. cloister 22. archer 24. cur 25. Germany 26. Asia 27. will 28. Erin 31. mini 32. antics 33. Italic 34. Cal 35. twine 36. October 42. outer 44. pantomime 45. past 47. able 50. imp 51. need 52. each 55. sure 57. ate 58. iced 59. type 60. Anna 61. reap 64. Dane 65. a skill 66. astral 67. yes 68. picnic

Down: 1. normal 2. wagers 3. eel 4. rot 5. berry 6. pens 8. boards 11. mere 13. cirrus 14. etch 18. leg 19. ore 20. tradition 21. royalist 22. academic 23. criminal 29. Rita 30. nil 32. act 36. orphan 37. tingle 38. boo 39. Roi 40. steam 41. trot 43. umpire 46. spic 48. beauty 49. edge 53. ascension 54. hydraulic 55. Saturday 56. replants 62. ease 63. per 65. Alp

Answers

HIS, HER AND OUR WORDS.

Whist, chisel, thistle, history, hisses, whistle.

Heron, sphere, cheroot, thermal, cherry, ether.

Four, flour, detour, courage, mourn, dour.

HIDDEN HOMOPHONES		ABC DIAMOND WORD PUZZLE	A RHYMING PUZZLE
1. Amiss	4. A miss	A	Brain
2. Acorn	8. A corn	R A	Insane
3. Ahead	3. A head	E A R	Reign
4. Abeam	6. A beam	R A K E	Drain
5. Ascent	9. A scent	B R E A K	Stain
6. Abound	1. A bound	B E A K E R	
7. Across	10. A cross	B R A K E	Frank
8. Averse	5. A verse	B A R E	Lank
9. Apart	7. A part	B A R	Yank
10. Alight	2. A light	A B	
11. About	12. A bout	B	Season
12. Affair	15. A fair	B A	Onion
13. Allot	14. A lot	C A B	Undone
14. Appoint	11. A point	C R A B	Tendon
15. Adore	13. A door	B R A C E	Harken
16. Assail	20. A sail	B R E A C H	
17. Accost	19. A cost	R E A C H	Idea
18. Accord	16. A cord	A R C H	Near
19. Atone	18. A tone	C A R	
20. Appeal	17. A peal	A C	Wrinkle
		C	Icicle
		D C	Nimble
		C A D	Thimble
		C L A D	Ethical
		L A C E D	Radical
		C A N D L E	
		D A N C E	
		D A N E	
		A N D	
		D A D	
		D	

AW, YER MOTHER'S AN AEROSOL SPRAY CAN!

The Great Balloon Race, London, Ontario.

Up, Up And Away:
History of the Balloon

by: Estelle Salata

photos: Ben Abruzzo, NFB Photothèque, National Museum of Science and Technology, Academy of Motion Picture Arts and Sciences.

Ever since the beginning of time, man has dreamt of flying. Greek and Roman mythology depicted gods and goddesses with wings. Icarus, according to Greek legend, wore wings of feathers and wax. When he flew too close to the sun, the hot sun melted the wax and Icarus plunged to his death. The Chinese invented the kite in 1000 B.C. *The Arabian Nights* tells the story of a king who flew on a magic carpet. Leonardo da Vinci drew many strange and wonderful flying machines after studying the flight of birds. None of the machines was ever built.

The first airship to leave the ground and take to the skies was not equipped with wings, nor did it resemble a bird. It was a hot-air balloon. The earliest recorded ascent of a hot-air balloon was that of a model invented by a Brazilian, Father Bartolomeu de Gusmao, in 1685. The model was flown indoors in 1709 in Portugal. A little more than half a century later, Joseph and Etienne Montgolfier were not searching for the key to unlock the mysteries of flight the day in 1782 that they began experiments in their paper making shop in Annonay, France.

"Smoke is lighter than air," Joseph mused aloud to his brother. "That's why it rises. I wonder what would happen if we filled a paper sack with smoke and let it rise."

On the brink of discovery, the Montgolfier brothers searched the shop for the finest quality paper they could find. They made a small sack, built a fire on the stone floor, and filled the sack with smoke. They watched it rise, hover above the fire, then lift to the ceiling. When it touched, it tipped over and fell to the floor.

Elated, they tried more experiments in the open air where they could build a bigger fire and use a larger sack. The first effort failed as the wind overturned it.

The brothers found a candle holder to act as a balance. They attached it to the mouth of the sack with strings. This time, the experiment worked perfectly. The sack climbed to an altitude of about thirty feet, then drifted with the wind before slowly descending to the ground. The first hot-air balloon in history had flown skyward.

They examined the sack and found it was still full of smoke. If the smoke hadn't caused the sack to soar, what had? Joseph Montgolfier reasoned that the air inside must remain hot in order for the balloon to fly. The brothers excitedly attached a brazier to the sack and this time it remained aloft for a longer period. They still didn't realize that it was the hot air and not the smoke that enabled the balloon to rise.

The King of France, Louis XVI, heard news of the experiments with a wonderful flying machine. He requested a demonstration at the Palace of Versailles. His Queen, Marie Antoinette, and the Court were present as the Montgolfier brothers unveiled their surprise. They had brought along the first space travellers — a duck, a rooster, and a lamb. The animals were tied into the gallery and sent aloft, quacking, crowing, and bleating! The balloon remained airborne for eight minutes, the reluctant passengers returning to earth safely. The King suggested that a prisoner be selected for the next demonstration. But Francois Pilatre de Rozier, a member of his Court, requested the honour. Thus, the first manned flight occurred on 15 October 1783. The gondola contained buckets of water and sponges. The brazier which kept the air hot had to be fed with chopped straw. Sparks igniting the balloon from the hot coals in the brazier kept the first aviator busy putting out small fires. The flight lasted four hours as the balloon strained against its moorings. Hot air in the balloon was allowed to cool gradually, and the vehicle was pulled back to earth.

Pilatre de Rozier and the Marquis d'Arlandes were the first two men to make a free flight through space in a Montgolfier hot-air balloon on 21 November 1783. The balloon, 75 ft. (23 m) high by nearly 50 ft. (15 m) in diameter,

was made of cloth backed with paper and heated by a furnace burning chopped straw.

A few weeks later Jacques Charles of France made the first ascent in a hydrogen filled balloon. The gas balloon proved to be superior to the hot-air type. The physicist sent up his unmanned hydrogen balloon from Paris where it flew for 15 miles (24 km) to Gonesse. Farmers working in the fields panicked when they saw the balloon. When it landed, they attacked it with pitchforks and tied it to the tail of a running horse!

But the great balloon race was on! The use of hydrogen balloons became the rage of adventurous men who dreamed of flight. Messrs. Charles and Robert made their first voyage in a hydrogen balloon. Charles had designed the balloon and one of Robert's brothers had designed the rubberised fabric. Modern ballooning derives from this "Charliere," as the balloon was called. It is fitted with a net, a car, a valve in the crown, ballast and a barometer to act as altimeter. They ascended from the gardens of the Tuileries in Paris, watched by a crowd of 400,000.

Many records were established and then broken as both men and women took to the air. On 4 October 1784 the first woman aeronaut, Madame Thible, ascended at Lyon in a hot-air

balloon with Fleurant as pilot. They sang to one another as they floated away. The first crossing of the English Channel by air was accomplished by Dr. John Jeffries and Jean Pierre Blanchard. The latter was one of the greatest of the earliest aeronauts, being the first to ascend in several countries. Pilatre de Rozier, two years after his successful first free flight in a Montgolfier balloon, became the first aerial fatality in history during an attempt to cross the English Channel. The first human parachute drop was made on 22 October 1797 by Andre-Jacques Garnerin from an unpiloted hydrogen balloon in Paris. The following year another French balloonist, Pierre Tetu-Brissy, made the first balloon ascent on horseback.

Ballooning became a popular spectator sport in the nineteenth century. The balloons were ornately decorated; draped and tasselled, with pictures painted in bright colours on the surface, they were beautiful works of art. The aeronauts were great showmen, who thrilled the crowds with spectacular displays. They waved flags from the gondolas and threw down brightly coloured streamers. Some, like Madame Blanchard, wanted to delight the audiences even further and lit fireworks from the air. Her plan backfired, however, and tragedy struck at the Tivoli Gardens in 1819. It is described in the book *The Conquest of the Air,* by Frank Howard and Bill Gunston:

In the lantern-lit, shadowy walks the crowd waited expectantly for the maroon that would signal the ascent . . . Madame Blanchard soared into the air, trailing beneath her car a great star of silver fire. Tremendous applause. Now brightness falls from the air. Madame has lit bombs of gold and silver rain, sending them floating earthwards on miniature parachutes. Renewed applause, presently redoubled as a great jet of flame shoots out of the balloon. Alas, this was no part of the performance, as was soon apparent. The port-fire Madame was using to ignite the fireworks had set light to the gas issuing from the neck of the ascending balloon . . . Madame Blanchard slid helplessly down the steeply pitched roof and plunged to her death upon the pavement below.

In July 1821 coal-gas was first used for inflating balloons by Charles Green in London. Green's first ascent was part of the coronation festivities of George IV of England. Charles F. Durant, the first great American aeronaut, made his first ascent on 9 September 1850 from Castle Gardens, New York.

Canada joined the world of flight one hundred years ago. On July 30, 1979 three men-Charles Page, Charles Grimley and Richard Cowan-left the ground of Montreal in a hydrogen-filled balloon. Ray Munro, another Canadian, presently holds 34 records for hot-air ballooning.

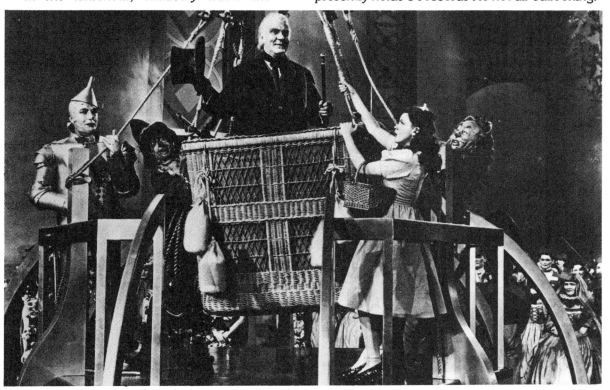

Double Eagle II, her crew and flight path.

in the skies today.

Balloons have continued to capture the imagination of adventurers, writers, movie makers, record breakers, and dreamers. When the troubles of the world become unbearable, the hero soars away in a balloon — the ideal means of getting away from it all. Balloons have competed with movie stars on the silver screen in several films, from the fantastic and light-hearted romance to the colossal epic of disaster. The wizard in "The Wonderful Wizard of Oz" rises aloft and floats innocently away, whereas the Goodyear Blimp is used to carry a horrible weapon in "Black Sunday."

A famous British balloon, *Jambo,* became the star attraction of several motion pictures, including "The Bed Sitting Room" in which two actors are borne aloft in an old police car. Albert Finney takes his leave of the world in *Jambo* at the end of the picture "Charlie Bubbles." *Jambo* also starred in "Those Magnificent Men in Their Flying Machines" in which there is a balloon musket duel.

In 1978 the first Atlantic crossing in a balloon, *Double Eagle II,* was made by three Albuquerque, New Mexico, businessmen — Max Anderson, Larry Newman, and Ben Abruzzo. The flight took 137 hours and six minutes, covering about 3,500 miles and ending in a wheat field near Miserey, France. It shattered the long standing distance and duration records for ballooning. The first attempt in 1977 had almost ended in disaster as the balloon went down and its two occupants, Anderson and Abruzzo, had to fight 25-foot-high waves off the coast of Iceland. Anderson intends to see China, Tibet, Nepal, the Himalayas, the Pacific and almost the entire world in 80 days from the gondola of a balloon. The trip is planned for 1981.

The balloon is unique in that it is the only aircraft to span the entire history of flight. Today there is a revival of interest in lighter-than-air flight. Balloon travel saves fuels derived from oil and does not seriously damage the environment. Evidence that the balloon will be used tomorrow for such purposes as recreational travel, inner-city travel, short trips or long cruises is an exciting futuristic concept. The history of the balloon has not yet come full circle.

The next step in the evolution of the balloon was the airship, a balloon powered by engines. When he climbed aboard his steam-driven, hydrogen-filled, 144-foot long creation, in Paris in 1852, Henri Giffard became simultaneously the pilot of the first powered aircraft and the first airship. He zoomed along at the impressive speed of 6 mph (10 kph) for 17 miles.

The final phase of the history of the balloon was the development of the dirigible. In 1900 Count Ferdinand von Zeppelin constructed a cigar-shaped rigid dirigible airship which was used in air raids against Britain during World War One. The dirigible was capable of being steered or guided, whereas in the early days of ballooning the navigator had to depend upon the whim of the wind. The huge airships became a popular means of transportation, carrying passengers great distances. The *Graf Zeppelin* logged more than a million miles, including 104 ocean crossings and the world's first-ever round-the-world air trip, in the eight years before her retirement in 1936. The *Hindenburg* was an aerial cruise ship with an 804-foot dining room, palatial lounges and 70 bedrooms. On 3 May 1937 the giant airship exploded while landing at Lakehurst, New Jersey, at the end of a transoceanic voyage from Germany. There were 97 passengers aboard; 36 were killed and many suffered horrible burns. This tragedy brought the era of the dirigible to an end. Only occasionally are the "forgotten giants" seen

"SUPER SKYTACULAR"
by: Estelle Salata

Look, up in the sky! It's a bird! It's a plane! It's "Super Skytacular," a dazzling display of disco lights twinkling and blinking in a magic lantern show of animated cartoons and messages. The four specially fitted Goodyear blimps are known as goodwill ambassadors of the air. Seventy-five per cent of the messages flashed to after-dark audiences below are public service announcements rather than advertisements.

"Super Skytacular" spectacles include a marching band, a baseball player slamming a line drive which almost decapitates the pitcher, a football player making good on a field goal attempt, a basketball player sinking a foul shot, and a golfer making a long drive to the green, then sinking his putt.

Special animated messages razzle-dazzle the night sky during the holiday seasons. A turkey meant for the Thanksgiving table escapes a man with an axe. A child lights a giant Fourth of July firecracker which explodes to form an American flag. Santa Claus, his sleigh and reindeer flash across the sky during the Yuletide season and the Magi and their camels follow the Star of Bethlehem.

A marvel of electronic engineering, the messages run on the sign are created on exotic electronic equipment in a special lab in Akron, Ohio. A technician "draws" the animation and copy on a cathode ray tube with a special "light beam" pencil. Then a computer takes over. The process results in a magnetic data tape.

A six-minute tape consists of 40 million pieces or bits of "on-off" information which, when run through special electronic readers aboard the airship, control lamp and colour selection and the speed at which messages are run.

Like its American sister ships, the Goodyear blimp *Mayflower* is named after a yacht which has won the America's Cup race. It is the smallest of the four Goodyear blimps fitted with skytacular panels. The "Super Skytacular" signs on each side of the *America*, *Columbia* and *Europa* are 105 feet long and 24.5 feet high. Each includes 3,780 lamps, or a total of 7,560 per ship. These specially designed lamps, inside red, blue, green and yellow reflectors, are connected by 80 miles of wiring.

On each ship there is only enough room in the gondola for the pilot and six passengers. Each of the three larger ships is staffed by a crew of 23, including five pilots, 17 ground crewmen and a public relations representative. Approximately 8,000 passengers are carried annually by each airship.

The blimps are in great demand by television networks for use as aerial camera platforms for special events such as the Super Bowl.

The next time you look up in the sky and think you see a flying saucer, you had better look twice. Perhaps it's one of the Goodyear blimps lighting up the night sky in all its galactic glory.

Gymnastics

by: Caroline M. Jackson   illustrations: Susan Cook   photos: John Bovard

So you would like to become a gymnast? Perhaps you watched Nadia Comaneci during the Olympic Games and were inspired. No doubt you were very impressed by her agility and wonderful precision. However, thinking of doing gymnastics and actually reaching such a level of proficiency are two different things!

Ask yourself a few questions. *Firstly,* is there a place nearby where you can train? Many recreation centres and some schools have excellent programmes, and there are private clubs. A gymnasium or a large hall is a prerequisite,

FLOOR AREA "A"

1   2   SPRING   RUN L-R-L

CURVING TOWARD CORNER "C"

3   HOP   ½ TURN   4   HOP   ½ TURN

although in the early stages a smaller area equipped with mats is excellent for practising novice tumbling.

Secondly, do you enjoy doing handstands and cartwheels, and do you have good natural balance and agility? School gym class will give you a good indication of your capabilities. Don't worry about not being particularly strong; this can be developed with time and workouts.

Thirdly, ask yourself if you have the ability to stick to an activity, even though you fail the first time. Gymnastics often means practising the same routine again and again until it is perfect, punctuated by occasional falls onto foam mats. "If at first you don't succeed, try again" is very much the gymnast's motto.

When beginning this sport, depending upon age and ability, the young gymnast will spend much time preparing for the exercises by practising on floor mats under the careful supervision of a coach. The groundwork is very important, and cartwheels, handstands, splits and back handsprings have to be learned on the mats before you encounter the beam, or else the results could be unfortunate! The body has to be in good condition, of course, before even attempting these exercises, and at the beginning and end of every session stretch and conditioning exercises MUST be practised to avoid unnecessary injury.

Here are some simple exercises you may practise for gymnastics:

(a) Sit on the floor with your legs apart in a V position. Lean forward and grasp one of your ankles or calves with your hands. Gently pull yourself forward as far as you can without straining. Hold for a short while, then slowly straighten. Now, do the same with the other leg. This exercise will improve your flexibility.

(b) Perhaps you would like to try the crab position. Lie on your back with both knees bent and feet as close to your body as possible (use bare feet if possible, so that you do not slip). Bring your hands, palm downwards, fingertips pointing towards your feet, close to the side of your neck. Push down on your hands until your body is raised from the floor and forms an arch. Try to rise onto your toes and hold the position for a short while before slowly relaxing back to your original position. (The next time you watch a gymnast perform either on floor or beam, observe how many times she goes through this position in a back or front walkover.)

(c) If you can do cartwheels, try to improve them with nice straight legs. Have a friend watch and tell you when they are bent. Try to do cartwheels beginning on the opposite arm. Not so easy? Most of us favour one direction, but a gymnast must be able to do it both ways. This exercise will improve your co-ordination and help strengthen your arms.

(d) Test your balance. Mark out a length of floor with masking tape and pretend this is your

STEP   STEP   LEAP   STEP

6

beam. Practise walking along its length, head held high with toes pointed. At each end practise turns, swivelling on the balls of your feet, and once you get more confident try some little hops. If you are doing well, try a cartwheel along the line placing *both* hands along the tape.

Once good conditioning has been achieved, the gymnast may use the apparatus while being spotted by either the coach or a trained fellow gymnast. When confidence is obtained, routines can be learned. At this point, provided a certain standard of proficiency has

been reached, the gymnast may wish to leave recreational and enter competitive gymnastics — in other words, compete with other clubs in the area. If this route is chosen, it will be necessary to participate in more practice sessions and, in the case of a female gymnast, perhaps complement her gymnastic activities with dance or ballet lessons. This is especially necessary for the floor routine, when she has to interpret music and execute very fine artistic movements.

Ladies Gymnastics includes four routines:

1. *Floor exercise:* following a dance format,

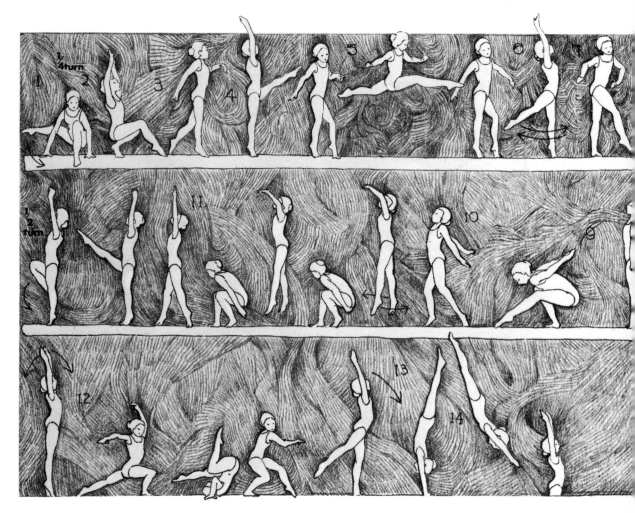

this routine includes leaps, jumps, walkovers and acrobatics, executed within a square area of mats and performed to music.

2. *Vault:* the gymnast uses a beat board for added height; there are many positions, from the simple "layout squat" to the advanced "tsukahara."
3. *Uneven Bars:* the gymnast has a routine of swing movements, incorporating frequent bar changes, and finishing with a dismount.
4. *Balance Beam:* the gymnast has to execute a series of turns and pivots, leaps and acrobatic elements on a beam 10 cm wide and 120 cm above the floor.

    Men's gymnastics requires six routines:

1. *Floor exercise:* a series of tumbling runs with scales, balances, held positions and acrobatic moves.
2. *Vault:* men jump the length of the vault; one of the more difficult vaults is the handspring front somersault.
3. *Parallel Bars:* (about 170 cm above the floor) a routine of swings passing through handstands. The gymnast must perform skills above as well below the bars.
4. *Side-horse:* the gymnast performs body circles and must cover all sections of the horse.
5. *Rings:* (suspended 2.7 metres off the floor.)

undergrasp

provided for spectators, a PA system and recorded music made available, invitations sent to other clubs and judges and scorers contacted for the event.

Judging: Each routine is worked out of a total of ten points. The score is based on a deduction system. For example, a fall would perhaps be a .5 deduction, a wobble on the beam a .2, etc.

Many other points are important. For example, *appearance* — the gymnast must be well-groomed with hair neatly tied back. Even if he or she is feeling nervous, a pleasant appearance — no frowns or displays of tension — is expected. *Rhythm* — free flowing movement with no hesitation is desired. *Full use* of the apparatus must be made: for example, when performing on the beam, a girl would lose points if she only used half the length. *Body extension* — there is no point in doing a floppy handspring; instead the body should be taut and spring-like.

Hopefully the next time you observe a gymnast in action, you will appreciate the hard work that went on behind the scenes. But better still, now that you have read about it, you may wish to strive for the beauty and grace which may be yours in the world of gymnastics.

A Sample Bar Routine
(Category: Midget and Argo — ages 8 to 12)
UNEVEN BARS:
1. *Stand under High Bar, facing Low Bar, overgrasp on Low Bar. With one foot take-off back hip pullover Low Bar to front support.*
2. *Immediate squat one leg through the arms. Change grasp to undergrasp.*
3. *Stride circle forward to catch High Bar with both hands.*
4. *Place one leg against Low Bar and bring the other leg straight to High Bar. Single leg kip to front support on High Bar, cast.*
5. *Back hip circle.*
6. *Immediate cast to straddle on High Bar, sole circle backwards, 1/2 turn, front wrap Low Bar.*
7. *Squat on Low Bar and immediately jump to straddle position on High Bar.*
8. *Sole circle backwards on High Bar to dismount under the High Bar.*

The gymnast must accomplish swinging moves without moving the rings. Two handstands are required and at least one move showing exceptional strength.

6. *High Bar:* (also 2.7 metres from the floor.) Movement consists almost entirely of swings down in straight body or handstand position. There must be frequent changes of direction and various grip changes.

Competitions in gymnastics are called "meets," and they are often organised in rotation by different clubs in an area. The gymnast, however, is not the only one who has to prepare for such competitions. A gymnasium has to be set up with apparatus, refreshments

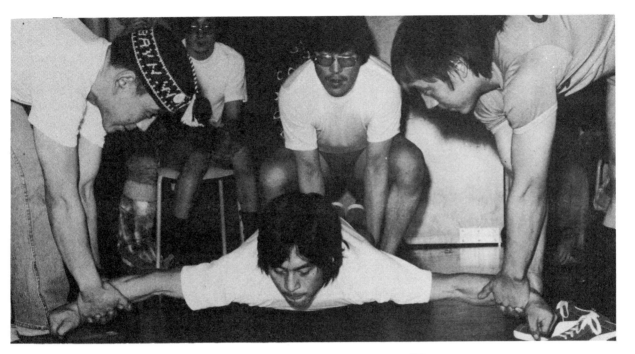

The Arctic Winter Games

by: Heather Kellerhals-Stewart
photos: Mike Van Duffelin

March may signal the coming of spring to southern Canada, but in the north it's the perfect time for holding the Arctic Winter Games. The days are lengthening and the sun is gradually growing warmer. Temperatures may still drop as low as -30°C. though, enough to make athletes and spectators grumble if opening speeches drag on too long!

Banners, drums and plenty of noise and excitement opened the first Arctic Winter Games at Yellowknife, Northwest Territories, in 1970. Since that time the games have been held every two years — Whitehorse, Yukon (1972), Anchorage, Alaska (1974), Schefferville, Québec (1976), and Hay River, Pine Point, NWT (1978). Glance at a map of northern Canada and you will get some idea of the tremendous distances athletes, coaches and officials have to travel. But one of the reasons for holding the Arctic Winter Games in the first place was to develop a feeling of unity by bringing together the many different peoples of this huge area — Inuit, Indian, French-speaking, English-speaking . . . Imagine too the difference between Anchorage, Alaska, a bustling seaport of around 150,000, and Schefferville, a small mining community of some 4,200 people on the edge of the tundra.

The idea of winter games is not new. Many years ago the Inuit people would gather together at the darkest, coldest time of the year for a festival of dancing, feasting and endurance tests. A large igloo was built for the occasion, but even then games or contests that needed much space were impractical.

Demonstrations of these traditional skills have become a part of the modern Arctic Winter Games. You can listen to the Mackenzie Delta Drum Dancers, watch a skilled soapstone carver at work, or perhaps see the champion at *ipirautaqurniq* (precision whip flicking) snap a toothpick loose from the sole of an assistant's shoe at a distance of 8 m. If none of these sound energetic enough for your liking, move on to another area where you can observe the top athletes from Alaska demonstrating their specialities. Here is one man, the champion at *aqraorak,* trying to kick a sealskin ball suspended from a high pole. With a tremendous effort he reaches 2.5 m. Nearby is another athlete prac-

tising the sport of *nalukataak.* Watch it! There he goes, bouncing as high as he can from a tightly stretched walrus hide held by several assistants.

Six of these traditional northern sports have become official events in the Arctic Winter Games: one and two foot high kick, kneel jump, airplane, one hand reach and rope gymnastics. The one hand reach is always a "crowd pleaser" because of the sheer strength and concentration it demands. The competitor must touch a hide-covered stick hanging above his head while balancing his body on one hand!

However, the Arctic Winter Games are really dominated by sporting events that sound more familiar to southern ears — basketball, badminton, volleyball, hockey, curling, wrestling, judo, shooting, figure skating, archery, boxing, table tennis and alpine skiing (where hills exist!). There is a biathlon event, in which competitors use hunting rifles and snowshoes to display a knowledge of traditional hunting skills. Two events that usually draw keen

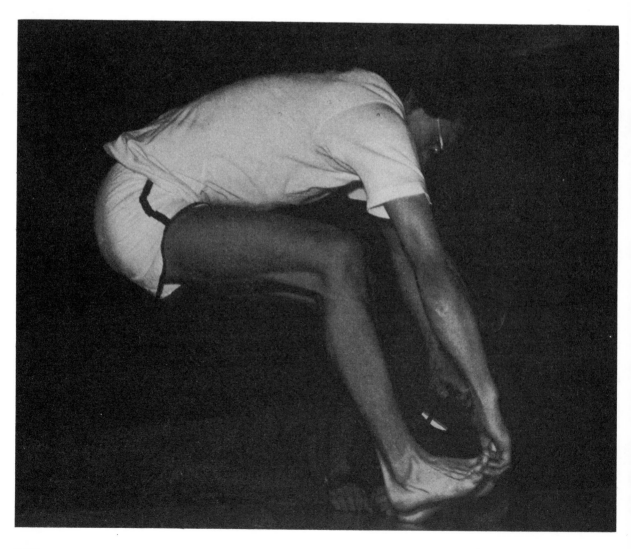

competitors from the smaller settlements are snowshoeing and cross country skiing.

Each of the four northern areas — Northwest Territories, Yukon, Nouveau Québec and Alaska — is responsible for sending a group of athletes to the Arctic Winter Games. This means many pre-game trials which give smaller communities a chance to join in the fun and competition, even if they do not make it to the "finals." Generally the larger centres like Whitehorse, Yellowknife and Inuvik end up with the winners, simply because of better coaching and facilities.

When the flags came down after the 1978 games in the neighbouring communities of Hay River and Pine Point on the southern shores of Great Slave Lake, Alaska had captured 62 gold *ulus* (medals shaped in the form of the traditional Inuit cutting knife), the Northwest Territories 27 and the Yukon 19. Nouveau Québec, the least populated of the four areas, has dropped out of competition temporarily to concentrate on local sporting events, but some people are already looking ahead to the time when the whole Northern polar area will be represented.

At the close of the games athletes began boarding planes that would take them to homes most southerners have only heard or read about — Dawson City, Inuvik, Pelly Crossing, Fort Simpson, Fairbanks. They were carrying away not only the coveted ulus, but memories of the new friendships they had made. There was the inevitable let down after the hectic week of fun and competition, but they had the next Arctic Winter Games to look forward to in 1980 at Whitehorse.

Ginkgo Biloba~The Oldest Tree On Earth

by: Eileen Cade-Edwards

illustrations: Steve LeBlanc

The *ginkgo* is the oldest of all living trees. Known botanically as *ginkgo biloba* ("biloba" meaning that its leaves have two lobes), it provided food for dinosaurs during the Mesozoic era. By studying fossilized ginkgo twigs and leaves found in rocks in many parts of the world, *paleobotanists* — scientists who study fossil plants — can trace the tree, in its present form, back over 150 million years!

It is the only survivor of a family of forest trees which existed 200 million years ago, at a time when true broad-leaved trees had not yet appeared. So, although the ginkgo is often classified as a conifer, it is actually more fern than anything else.

If you examine a leaf closely you will notice that it is quite unlike one from any other tree. It is fan-shaped and fan-veined, and the texture is thick and leathery. In China this tree is sometimes called "duck-foot" (*yah chio*); when the leaves turn golden yellow in the autumn they really do resemble the webbed feet of a duck. The ginkgo is also known in China as "silver apricot" (*yin-hing*), because of the edible fruit it bears.

Before the coming of the glaciers and extreme changes in the climate, the ginkgo had grown freely in most areas of the world, but like many other prehistoric animals and plants it gradually disappeared. Until 300 years ago, paleobotanists firmly believed the tree to be extinct. And it was — almost!

In 1690 a very excited botanist named Dr. Engelbert Kaempfer reported that he had found the ginkgo alive and well, growing in a

Japanese temple garden. A single leaf from those he collected at that time can be seen in the British Museum of Natural History. And since Dr. Kaempfer's discovery the ginkgo has begun to spread again, but this time as a planted tree.

The ginkgo is a hardy specimen. It will grow in almost any kind of soil, in temperatures as low as -34.0 degrees Celsius. It is immune to nearly all pests and diseases and it will tolerate cramped conditions, city soot and fumes.

If you know someone who owns a ginkgo and will spare you a slip, you can grow your own little tree with very little trouble. You will need:

— a large juice can
— equal quantities of peat moss and coarse sand to fill it
— a stake about 1-1/2 times the length of the slip to be rooted
— a large clear non-porous plastic bag
— a rubber band

— a little rooting hormone (obtainable from most garden centres)
— the slip from your friend's ginkgo (pull a small twig away from a bough so that it comes away in a "heel.")
— plus a lot of patience, as this is a slow-growing tree at first!

To plant your ginkgo:

1. Make four or five holes in the bottom of the can for drainage.
2. Fill the can with the peat moss-sand mixture (Fig. 1).
3. Remove lower leaves of ginkgo slip. Dip lower half-inch of stem in rooting hormone.
4. Make a hole 76 mm (3 in.) deep in the centre of the soil mixture and carefully place slip in the hole, pressing the soil up around it fairly tightly to prevent movement (Fig. 2).
5. Press stake into soil beside the slip — but not too close — and tie stake and slip together (Fig. 3).

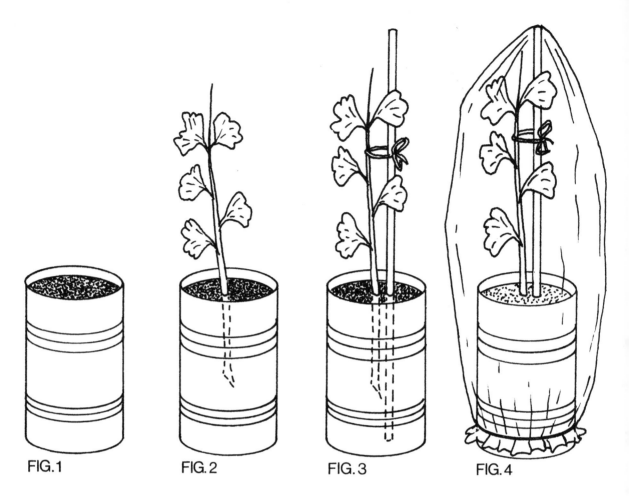

FIG. 1 FIG. 2 FIG. 3 FIG. 4

6. Water well.

7. Cover with plastic bag and secure around base of can with rubber band (Fig. 4).

Condensation will soon form on the inside of the plastic bag; this is as it should be. If moisture should disappear it may mean the bag is torn. If so, water the tree again and repair the tear with tape.

In about eight weeks, remove the plastic bag and the stake with care. (Don't worry if all the leaves fall off the slip.) With the edge of a blunt knife loosen the soil around the edge of the can and very gently transfer the contents (soil and all) into a ready-made hole in the open ground, where you wish your ginkgo to grow. The ideal time to plant is as soon after the end of June as possible, to allow plenty of time for a good root system to develop before winter. Water often, but do not disturb the tree.

You are now the proud owner of a ginkgo. Granted, it is a tiny one, but with care it will grow into a large and beautiful tree. Ideal fodder for your pet dinosaur!

Kristi

by: Marilyn Scheske   illustrations: Mary Trach

Kristi sat on the grey steps beside her house. The cement felt warm against her bare legs. She watched an ant carrying a bread crumb. My bread crumb, she thought. Her uneaten sandwich lay on her lap.

Kristi rested her chin in her hands. Her hands smelled like school — chalk and dust and sweat all mixed together. She looked across the street. The weeping willow tree in Mr. Grant's yard looked blurry. Kristi shut her eyes tight but one tear escaped and rolled down her cheek. She stuck out her tongue and let a tear slither on to it. The tear had a salty taste.

Kristi could see the other kids walking home from school in twos and threes. She saw her best friend LeeAnn walking with Susan. Kristi had walked home alone. She had been home for a long time. Everyone else had stayed at school to skip.

Skipping. That was the problem. Kristi couldn't skip. She didn't know why. There was nothing wrong with her. She looked down at her legs, already beginning to turn a brownish colour from the sun. Her legs were strong. They could run and jump and walk, but they couldn't skip. She had tried and tried.

It looked so easy when you watched. The rope came over your head and you jumped over it. Simple. But when Kristi managed to get the rope over her head it wouldn't go under her feet, and if it went under her feet it wouldn't go over her head.

At first it was funny, and Kristi laughed too. Everyone was learning. But suddenly Kristi realized that everyone else had learned and she hadn't. And it was the skipping season. That's all anybody every did. And if you couldn't skip in a skipping world, you might as well stay at home.

Kristi began to stay in bed longer in the mornings. She didn't get up when her mother called her. That way she could leave for school later, and maybe get there just in time for the bell to ring. At recess she would ask the teacher if she could erase the boards and put out the workbooks for the next class, and after school she would race home alone. When she lay in bed at night, she could hear skipping rhymes repeating over and over in her head:

Popeye, Popeye, sick in bed,
Called for the doctor and this is what he said,
Take two steps forward, turn around —
Do the hokey-pokey and get out of town.

Kristi asked for a new skipping rope. A pink one like LeeAnn's. Maybe that would help.

It didn't.

She tied a skipping rope to a pillar in the basement and begged her brother to turn.

His arms got tired.

Kristi practiced and practiced. She practiced until her legs ached and her arms were stiff.

"Oh Mom," she cried, "I'm going to have to be a never-ender for the rest of my life! And I don't *like* being the never-ender!"

Kristi's friend LeeAnn was now becoming the best skipper in the whole school.

She could do the egg beater and the double dutch and the dwarf and she knew all the verses and she *never* went out.

Kristi watched her. She looked her over from top to toe. There was nothing different about LeeAnn. Except that her sneakers were different from anybody elses.

"Maybe that's the secret," she thought. Kristi grinned to herself. She raced home after school.

"Mom," she called out as she threw the door open. "I need new sneakers. And I need them right away. For school. The red kind with the white stripe. Can we buy them tonight?"

Kristi bought new sneakers. The red kind with the white stripe. She tried them on. They felt good. She walked around her room with them. They felt springy. They made her feel like running and jumping and . . . skipping? Kristi could hardly wait until school the next day.

The next morning Kristi woke up early. She didn't wait to be called. From her bed she could see the new sneakers eyeing her. She flew out of bed and tried them on.

"Maybe they're magic sneakers," she thought to herself. "And when I try to skip in them, I will go soaring away into the sky and everybody will say, 'Look at Kristi! Look at Kristi!'

And I will wave at them and my red sneakers will gleam in the sun!"

Kristi ate her breakfast and hurried off to school. She could see LeeAnn and some of the other girls standing beside the school.

"Probably lining up to skip," Kristi said to herself. "And this time I'll be lining up, too. No more never-ending for me!" Her stomach felt fluttery and she ran faster.

But as Kristi got closer, she could see that the girls weren't lining up to skip at all. They were huddled in little groups.

"Hi, Kristi," called LeeAnn. "Did you bring your jacks?"

"My jacks?" asked Kristi, "Aren't we going to skip?"

"No," said LeeAnn. "We're tired of skipping. We're playing jacks now. Can you bring your double set at noon?"

"Okay," said Kristi. "I'll bring my double jacks."

Kristi looked down at her new red sneakers and grinned. She had been absolutely right. They were magic sneakers.

"I'll start with the onesies," she said as she sat down on the cement beside her best friend LeeAnn.

The Mummy Of Mammoth Cave

by: Robert F. Nielsen   *illustration: Susan Cook*

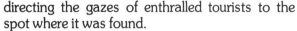

Lost John doesn't say much.

In fact, he hasn't said a word for 2300 years.

Ever since the accident . . .

Lost John is "The Mummy of Mammoth Cave." Or rather, the current edition; there have been others. The first, discovered in nearby Mummy Cave in 1813, was exhibited in Mammoth Cave for two years. Christened "Fawn Hoof," and referred to lovingly as "Kentucky's posthumous belle," when she was removed to a museum visitors to the cave were unhappy. To pacify them, Mammoth Cave guides began to display the "Mummy Seat," and to embellish Fawn Hoof's story. She was sometimes referred to as an Indian princess or queen, and some guides even invented a mummified child for her,

directing the gazes of enthralled tourists to the spot where it was found.

One thing was certain — Mammoth Cave was badly in need of another mummy to fill Fawn Hoof's moccasins. They found one; "Little Alice," discovered in 1875 in Salts Cave, was enlisted as the next "Mummy of Mammoth Cave," although the public was led to believe that Fawn Hoof had returned. Alice sojourned elsewhere for periods of time, but she devoted most of her days to thrilling and chilling the clientele at Mammoth

Cave. In 1922 she was billed as: "The Lady of the Cave. The little girl turned to stone; the most interesting and wonderful of all cave phenomena; a little girl, petrified or mummified by the action of the cave air . . . It is believed that the little girl had been captured by Indians, and rather than endure their torture she sacrificed her life." Brave words, but a baker's dozen years later, Alice was doomed to be upstaged.

In 1935 the discovery of another "Mummy of Mammoth Cave" — actually *in* Mammoth Cave for a change! — was timely; Alice was getting a bit shop-worn — both legs were broken and her skin was torn. Not, really, quite the glamour girl she had been in the good old days. She was retired to the bottom shelf in a room of an old out-of-the-way museum.

Lost John had been the victim of a tragic accident. One day the Indian miner had entered Mammoth Cave in search of gypsum, a white, brittle mineral used by the Indians to manufacture body paint. Fully two miles into the cave, Lost John discerned, by the dim light of his reed torch, an abundance of gypsum on the underside of a huge limestone rock perched on a ledge twenty feet above the floor of the cave. John picked up a small piece of limestone for a hammer, climbed to the ledge, and began to bang away. Beside him he placed extra torches and his lunch of hickory nuts.

Somehow, a small rock supporting the large one was dislodged — perhaps John inadvertently kicked it — and . . . Well, John was crushed to death.

For over two thousand years the constant temperature and humidity of Mammoth Cave did their eerie work on the corpse of Lost John, until 1935 when he was finally discovered. This was an important year in the history of Mammoth Cave; it had just been purchased by the people of Kentucky for a national park. Along came two guides, searching for a safe route for a tourist trail through the cave. Noticing a ledge previously unexamined, they made the ascent. Protruding from beneath an enormous boulder was the top of a human head . . .

Although he was the seventh mummy discovered in the local caves, John was the only one which scientists could examine in its original location. He was accorded the respect due a priceless gift from man's past; here was a glorious opportunity to learn the secrets of a long-lost civilization.

Eventually they had to get John out from under six tons of rock. Experts were summoned to wrap the stone in steel cables and erect strong supports from which to hang chain hoists. Gingerly the boulder was lifted and gently Lost John was taken from the scene of his demise. He was subjected to further intense inspection including radiocarbon dating which placed him away back in the fourth century B.C. A man of about forty-five, John was five feet three and a half inches tall. His present skin colour was a dark greyish-brown, its texture approximating that of a football. Around his wizened neck he wore a single polished mussel shell, and his only clothing was a skimpy woven garment.

Lost John is now a star attraction at Mammoth Cave. Displayed for all to see in a glass coffin near the natural entrance to the cave, he gives to each visitor the added fillip of being able to brag thereafter, "I saw the Mummy of Mammoth Cave!"

But Little Alice, now forgotten, jumped back into the limelight briefly. It seems that during all those years of being stared at by goggle-eyed tourists, she had been harbouring her little secret. Finally, to the scientists of the University of Kentucky, she revealed it.

You see, Little Alice is really a boy!

1. Owl
2. Eagle
3. Hawk
4. Nuthatch
5. Swallow
6. Heron
7. Mallard
8. Tit
9. Geese
10. Loon
11. Sparrow
12. Puffin
13. Knot
14. Snipe
15. Lark
16. Hummingbird
17. Robin
18. Thrush